MICKEY ROURKE

MICKEY ROURKE
Wrestling with Demons

SANDRO MONETTI

Dorset County Library	
Askews	2009
B/ROU	£18.99

R
OKS

First published in Great Britain in 2009 by
JR Books, 10 Greenland Street, London NW1 0ND
www.jrbooks.com

A catalogue record for this book is available from the British Library.

ISBN 978-1-906779-51-1

1 3 5 7 9 10 8 6 4 2

Printed by MPG Books, Bodmin, Cornwall

Contents

About the Author

Sandro Monetti is one of the world's most experienced and respected showbiz writers. The British journalist is based in Beverly Hills, California, from where he covers the Hollywood scene for the international press and moderates Q&As with movie stars for BAFTA-LA. During a 20-year career, he has worked for major media organisations like Sky TV, *News of the World* and the BBC.

Over that time, Sandro has followed Mickey Rourke's roller-coaster career as both reporter and fan. He also gives masterclass lectures to journalism students, directs acclaimed short films, part-owns a football club and co-hosts a podcast at www.2britsinla.com. His favourite Mickey Rourke films are *A Prayer for the Dying* and *The Wrestler*.

Preface

'**M**ost people are never lucky enough to hang out with their heroes, but tonight I'm so fortunate to share the stage with someone who has greatly inspired and entertained me for years. Ladies and gentlemen . . . Mickey Rourke!'

With those words, I introduced the comeback king of Hollywood at a Q&A following the BAFTA-LA screening of his life-changing movie *The Wrestler*. The large crowd got to its feet, clapping and cheering, giving an almost deafening ovation to show huge appreciation and sweet affection for a star who is only now receiving the recognition his immense talent deserves.

Every year, during what Hollywood calls 'awards season', I interview the big movie stars in the running for the film industry's glittering prizes at special screenings held for the various groups who vote for these awards. The likes of Cate Blanchett, Javier Bardem, Philip Seymour Hoffman and the rest would take their turn talking to me and the audience about their prestigious projects. But it always seemed like someone was missing from this annual glory circuit and that was the most utterly mesmerising and intriguing actor of his generation.

When Mickey Rourke burst on to the scene 25 years or so ago, and made an instant impact in movies like *9½ Weeks* and *Rumble Fish*, he was widely hailed as the most exciting new acting talent since James Dean or Marlon Brando. Fans like me certainly thought so and expected a string of Oscars, BAFTAs and blockbusters to follow. But a self-destructive tendency of almost Shakespearian proportion meant it didn't work out like that.

A succession of disastrous choices derailed his Hollywood career and left him looking like a washed-up has-been who would never return to the big time. His reputation for fighting with producers, showing up late to sets, not sticking to the script, bad-mouthing colleagues and raising hell wherever he went served to burn all his bridges in Tinseltown.

He then made the extraordinary decision to change careers and become a professional boxer. Mickey won his fights but lost his Hollywood looks, with the features that made him famous battered to a pulp. Some freaky facial surgery didn't help matters either. After retiring from the ring, a need for cash motivated his return to acting but a succession of dud films looked to have finished him off for good. He had two broken marriages behind him, lost his brother to cancer, was all alone in the world and had nothing going for him except his enduring talent.

But there's still magic in the Hollywood hills and sometimes it only takes one or two great performances to turn an actor's fortunes around and put him back on top. First came his stunning supporting role as tough but tender vigilante Marv in 2005's *Sin City*. Then, late in 2008, the buzz about Mickey's lead performance in a low-budget but high-quality new movie *The Wrestler* – sparked by glowing reviews and film festival prizes – rapidly grew into a crescendo that screamed from the rooftops one loud and clear message: 'Mickey is back!'

The title character he plays, Randy 'the Ram' Robinson, a once-great wrestler now seemingly past his prime and beaten down by life but looking for a return to the big time, has so many parallels with Mickey's own roller-coaster life that it's hard to see where the character begins and the man playing him ends.

The critics all raved about his career-reviving performance and, as he did the rounds of press conferences, Q&As and personal appearances to promote the movie, Mickey not only found himself in the running for the next Best Actor Oscar but also came to learn there had been a silent army of Mickey Rourke fans out there now emerging from the shadows to shake his hand and share their enthusiasm for his current success.

I was one of those devoted enthusiasts. As an international showbiz reporter for Britain's biggest newspapers, I have covered Mickey's headline-hitting career for two decades, attending his countless entertaining press conferences around the globe. As a fan, I bought tickets to his fights, became a frequent customer at the tiny café he used to own and eagerly went to see every single one of his films – even those most people have never heard of, like *Picture Claire*, *Fall Time* and the killer insect movie *They Crawl*.

For those of us who had followed his career so closely, it was a great thrill when *The Wrestler* saw this dazzling and charismatic performer rebound from the wilderness to the big time.

And so it was that, as one of the actors in contention for honours that year, he set foot on the awards circuit and our paths crossed, for the first time in years, at the British Academy of Film and Television Arts LA screening of *The Wrestler*. Mickey didn't disappoint and was everything I expected – tall and solid, moving with a tough guy swagger, shaking hands with sausage-like fingers and showing up with a little dog and a large entourage. The dog was Loki, a 17-year-old chihuahua who had become his constant companion, and the lively entourage included action star Jason Statham, model Lisa Snowdon and wrestling legend Rowdy Roddy Piper. Mickey was flamboyantly dressed, as usual, and I was, too – which prompted my hero to greet me with the words, 'Have you been raiding my closet?'

Equally fascinated to see the once down-and-out actor who had suddenly become Hollywood's darling again, the packed crowd hung on his every word as Mickey related his comeback tale to me on stage. He then graciously answered all the audience questions and seemingly shook every hand as the event ran way over time – but not a single person left before the end.

Off stage, Mickey and I talked more about how far he's come and what an extraordinary life he's had. It's been quite a journey . . . and I hope you'll enjoy reading about it over these following chapters.

Wrestling with Demons uncovers many fresh and fascinating stories about one of the most colourful figures in film history. From the night he set his home on fire to the day he trembled while having his ears pierced, it's all here, along with behind-the-scenes revelations from his films, including the movie he made in return for a paper bag stuffed with cash and the film for which he got into character by boarding a plane dressed as a woman.

Written with affection and insight but at the same time pulling no punches, this book aims to be a worthy tribute to, and an entertaining document of, a turbulent life lived from one huge drama to another by a bewitching actor who is as talented as he is troubled.

Mickey, thanks for the memories and all the great moments still to come.

Sandro Monetti

1

The Nightmare Years

Desperate, broken down and battered by setbacks, **Mickey** Rourke slumped to his knees in a New York church and prayed to a wooden sculpture of St Jude for the strength to stop himself doing what he was about to do. He had come to 42nd Street's Church of the Holy Cross one damp, dreadful day in the mid-1990s feeling at his lowest ebb and looking for guidance from, appropriately, the patron saint of lost causes.

With his movie acting career all washed up, his money gone and his wife, Carré Otis, walking out on him, Mickey was tormented by both suicidal and murderous thoughts.

He had a pistol in his pocket and a revenge plan in mind to do some serious harm to a man he says attacked his estranged wife – and, after that, he'd maybe turn the gun on himself.

The pain in his head felt unbearable as he reflected on the mess his life had become and how he had driven away the beautiful woman he loved so much. Mickey took from his other pocket a handwritten letter of apology he had written to Carré. Reading the sad note over and over again, he wondered if these would be the last words he would ever write.

Then he suddenly felt a reassuring hand on his shoulder. He turned around and looked into the kindly eyes of parish priest Father Peter Colapietro, who was used to seeing despairing down-and-outs show up at the rundown, red-brick church. On this occasion, though, he immediately recognised this tormented soul as the fallen movie star who a decade earlier had been one of Hollywood's biggest names, thanks to films like *9½ Weeks*, *Rumble Fish* and one that the priest had seen 15 times, *Angel Heart*.

Father Peter had Mickey tell him his troubles and then got him to hand over the gun after asking: 'Where in the Bible does it say, "Vengeance is mine, says Mickey Rourke"?' They lit a candle together and the priest assured the actor, long a man of faith, that God would give him the strength he needed. Father Peter watched Mickey fold and carefully place the note to Carré behind St Jude's statue and then led him to the rectory where he started a conversation with the desolate star, gently asking what had led him to such a dark place in his life.

It was a story that started only a few miles away across New York but left a legacy of pain that has stayed with Mickey forever.

■　■　■

Mickey Rourke has not had a birthday party since he was six. That was the year his parents split up, and he's not felt like celebrating since then. He has described his upbring-ing as 'unusual, crazy and violent' and says if he had the choice of living his childhood all over again, he would rather not have been born.

Life was a struggle from the start for Philip Andre Rourke who, just like his character in *The Wrestler*, Robin Robinson, avoids using his given name. He came to be known as Mickey due to a combination of his family's Irish ancestry (the ancestors came from Cork) and his father being a huge fan of baseball star Mickey Mantle.

Mickey Rourke was born in Schenectady, New York, on 16 September 1956 according to his official biography, although other sources, including police arrest records and school files in Miami, state he entered the world in 1952. Many actors shave a few years off their age to avoid being considered too old for certain roles, but Mickey may have confused a few other biographical details, too, more of which later.

His earliest memories were of constant rows between his mother Ann, a housewife and sometime nurse, and his father, also called Philip, who was an imposing figure. He was an amateur bodybuilder who had held the Mr New York title. Working as a carpenter, groundskeeper and janitor at the local golf club, he spent his free time either lifting weights or lifting a beer glass.

Mickey was closer to his dad and loved how big and strong he was. He loved touching his father on the upper arm as a signal to Phil, who would delight the boy by immediately then flexing his muscle to show him. The young Mickey was a funny-looking kid back then with big protruding ears and his appearance gave no hint that he would grow up to become a heart-throb movie star. Those ears seemed forever to be picking up the painful sound of his parents' conflict.

Phil and Ann would have many loud and violent arguments and their bust-ups often got too much for young Mickey who would run downstairs and take sanctuary in the basement apartment of his maternal grandmother. He frequently sat on the faded couch in front of her TV set, watching his favourite show, *The Little Rascals*, with a plate of homemade cookies at his side, trying to shut the anger upstairs out of his mind.

Things eventually reached breaking point in the marriage, with his mother and grandmother moving out and taking Mickey, his younger brother Joey and little sister Patti to start a new life with them in Miami. The children were initially told they were just going on a sunshine holiday and their father would join them in Florida in due course.

But the night before Ann left home, Phil took Mickey aside and told him he would never be coming home because his mother was splitting up the family. The boy felt furious, let down, confused and resentful. Unable then to grasp the complexities of adult relationships, he was extremely unhappy with his mother for taking him away. He didn't want to go but had no choice and his mood wasn't helped when he found himself moving from motel to motel after their arrival in Miami.

His mother eventually took over a launderette there and the family lived in the back rooms. Mickey started a new school nearby but had no interest in lessons and spent his time daydreaming rather than studying. He missed his dad and often kept with him an old black-and-white photograph of Phil in a bodybuilding pose – both arms raised and muscles pumped. It was the only glimpse of his father he would have for two decades.

As if the new surroundings weren't unsettling enough, just a year after the big move his now divorced mother got married again. She wed a widowed police detective called Gene Addis who provided Mickey with five older step-brothers. But Mickey didn't want anyone taking his father's place. 'A year . . . a year!' he would say incredulously. He is ashamed to say that he gradually came to call Gene 'Daddy', but theirs wasn't a happy relationship.

When he was eight years old, his school class were all making Valentine cards to take home to their parents and Mickey got so upset that his teacher eventually told him he didn't have to write 'To Dad' on his.

The joining of the Addis and Rourke clans sounded like the set-up in the classic US TV sitcom *The Brady Bunch*. But the way Mickey remembers life back then, it was more like living in the Manson family. Gene was strict with him, Joey and Patti, just as he was with his own children. But Mickey hated his tough guy ways. He quickly came to loathe his stepfather and has claimed on several occasions that he was bullied and beaten by the man he calls 'the violent cop who screwed me up'.

Mickey has often been close to tears when relating the tale of abuse he claims he suffered at Gene's hands, saying, in various interviews, 'it was like *Halloween 3*' and that he was the victim of 'nightmarish atrocities'. But he refuses to say exactly what abuse he suffered – except that it wasn't sexual – and insists he will only share that private information with the therapist who has been helping him come to terms with his past.

Hitting children to keep them in line was a lot more common back then in the 1960s than in these politically correct times but Gene Addis, who is now 81, still living in Miami and divorced from Mickey's mother, insists he was never abusive, just a strict disciplinarian.

He says Mickey has exaggerated his past but he loves him, always has done, and wishes he would get back in touch. But Mickey has had nothing to do with him for years and has no plans to change that state of affairs.

Mickey is also estranged from his mother, who now has Alzheimer's disease and lives in a care home. He could never get over how Ann would turn a blind eye and a deaf ear to his complaints about all the bad treatment he was receiving from her new husband.

The star cut off communication with her for a long time after he first started making money in movies and she requested that he buy her a $150,000 house. Their talking ceased for good after the death of his brother Joey, who had also resented her for breaking up the family.

While his brother, who fixed motorbikes, and sister, who became a beautician, would remain in Mickey's life, that wasn't the case with his stepbrothers. He never felt close to them. As kids, the boys would sleep in the same room in triple-decker bunk beds and, whenever Mickey fell out of his top bunk, which happened a few times, his step-brothers would all laugh at him.

Their tastes were completely different, too. His step-brothers absolutely loved wrestling and would go and watch the sport all the time. But Mickey had a terrible disdain for it and wouldn't change his mind about the sport until starring in *The Wrestler* four decades later.

Brother Joey and sister Patti seemed to adapt better to the new environment than Mickey. He craved the love and support of his mother but resented the way she was sharing her time and attention with her new husband and stepchildren. His grandmother was always there with a comforting arm around the shoulder or a loving smile but, apart from that, the lad felt largely lost and bewildered. He would rather have lived in a prison than in that house.

So Mickey simply retreated and lived in his head. He felt he was living in a family that was beyond dysfunctional and remembers walking along the street one day thinking, 'What am I doing living with these weird people?'

The frustration finally poured out of him when he had his first fistfight at the age of ten. Another boy at school came over and started kicking him in the playground. Mickey, a quiet and submissive child up until that point, suddenly snapped and started raining blows on his tormentor, giving him a severe beating. He might not have been able to strike back at home, but he decided from then on to wage war on anybody who picked on him elsewhere.

Depressed by his home life and feeling out of place in school, the youngster took to spending time on the streets. These were bleak times which he remembers as 'my nightmare years'. Searching for the feeling of belonging he failed to find at home, young Mickey took to hanging out with a gang of hard-up local kids, started dressing the way they did and became part of their street urchin, petty criminal lifestyle. Like his new pals, he developed a defiance of authority and total inability to conform, which meant he was always getting into trouble, especially with the teachers at school. He got into lots of fights and once took revenge on five young thugs who had beaten up his brother Joey by hunting each of them down separately and giving them a battering in return. Mickey would continue to be protective of Joey for many years, always paying his medical bills and getting him the best treatment as his little brother fought a long battle against cancer.

But back then, Mickey was doing too much scrapping in the streets for the liking of his disciplinarian stepdad. Gene felt he needed to find another outlet for the lad's aggression. So, in a bid to keep his 12-year-old stepson out of trouble, he signed him up for boxing lessons at Miami's world-famous Fifth Street Gym where the great Muhammad Ali trained for his world title fights.

No matter what wrongs Gene may have done Mickey, this particular idea was a master stroke. The lad was immediately seduced by the fight scene and soon decided to take up amateur boxing. Over the next few years, he fought in the Police Athletic League, a common starting point for young American boxers, as a 146lb welterweight, sometimes under the name Andre Rourke and at others as 'Mick the Slasher'. He displayed real talent for the sport and claims to have KO'd 12 consecutive opponents in the first round on his way to compiling an amateur boxing record of 20 wins, 17 by knock-out, and just 6 defeats – 4 as a result of disqualifications and 2 by lost decisions – while never being knocked out.

I say 'claims' because several sources believe Mickey has exaggerated his amateur boxing achievements in Florida and the available records don't go back that far to allow his fight statistics to be checked.

Mickey also claims to have spent part of his childhood in Liberty City, a tough Miami ghetto known for its slums, drugs and riots. His stepfather, however, claims they never lived there. Local telephone directories from Mickey's teenage years place the family in a far more pleasant and affluent area of Miami at the corner of Prairie Avenue and 47th Street.

What is undoubtedly true is that Mickey found a real passion for boxing and saw the sport as a chance to release all the anger that had been bubbling away inside him. It was around this time that he began to imagine a future for himself as a professional boxer. He had certainly learned from the best. During the five years he spent training at the Fifth Street Gym, Mickey watched Muhammad Ali at close quarters, learning many masterful moves by studying the champion he, and many others, believe to be the greatest boxer who has ever lived. He started to try and mimic Ali's 'float like a butterfly, sting like a bee' style in the ring.

His fascination with the boxing legend continued outside the gym. He would watch Ali doing morning training runs on a nearby golf course and, at nights, the teenager would go to Wolfie's coffee shop in South Beach and look on, star-struck, as the champ ate with fellow boxers such as Jerry Quarry and Jimmy Ellis.

Ali noticed his young fan hanging around and one day gave Mickey a much-prized present – a pair of his shorts that he had worn in the ring. Young Mickey couldn't believe it. He treasured the white satin trunks with gold stripes down the side and resolved to keep the priceless gift forever. So he wasn't exactly pleased to find his mother had thrown them away during a clear out a few days later because they were covered in blood. His subsequent confrontation with Ann marked the first time Mickey ever swore at his mother.

But his stepfather continued to be the main focus of his rage. Following all his workouts at the gym, Mickey had the strength and the skills to stand up to Gene. But although they continued to argue, it never ended with the future film star and fighter punching him out. The closest they came was when Mickey was 16 and in the throes of an especially blazing row with Gene at home. His stepdad challenged Mickey to step outside and fight him like a man, but the youngster declined the invitation.

While it was the opportunity he had long wanted, Mickey reasoned that his 146lb frame was no match for Gene, who was well over 200lb and, being good with his hands, could do him some serious damage in a proper fight. Mickey regrets he didn't even try to let him have it back then. It could be argued he has been unloading his anger at Gene ever since.

He went back to the gym and worked towards his dream of making it as a professional boxer. But his unprofessional attitude let him down. It gradually became clear that while Mickey loved the sport and possessed impressive ring skills, he just didn't have the discipline and commitment needed. He would stay out all night getting wasted. When he went to the gym and his trainer asked if he had been out on his daily morning run, Mickey would lie to him that he had, when, in actual fact, he had only just stumbled in after long hours partying with pals.

It was a health scare which eventually persuaded Mickey to throw in the towel on his boxing dreams. He suffered two concussions – one while sparring in 1969 with Cuban former world welterweight champion Luis Rodriguez and another when competing in a 1971 tournament for promising amateur fighters. Mickey was spooked by what happened to him after those incidents. He would find himself standing in the street suddenly not knowing where he was going.

After the second concussion, doctors told him to take a year off from the sport and rest. His trainer wanted him to continue with boxing after that and move to the great fighting city of Philadelphia to improve his boxing skills. But the fear of permanent brain damage put him off a career in the ring. Mickey decided to give up boxing and look for something else to do with his life.

Had he stuck with boxing, Mickey says he would never have become an actor. But the decision to give up the sport was one he would nevertheless regret. It troubled him for years – so much so, that he would make an unlikely return to the ring two decades later.

Mickey had been a good American football player at school but decided to give up that contact sport, too, in view of his boxing injury. He had no future prospects, either, in the other sport in which he excelled – baseball – having blown his big chance when some big league talent scouts visited the school looking for new players.

Mickey's performances at first base really caught the eye – so much so that he was asked to coach the younger kids at school, and one of the juniors under his wing was future movie star Andy Garcia. But the fact that Mickey never made the progress he should have done in playing the sport was primarily down to his problem with authority figures. If anyone over 30 told him to do something, he invariably wouldn't do it.

One of those authority figures was his baseball coach, the highly respected Skip Bertman, who had brought long-hoped-for success to the school team and would go on to be voted into the sport's Hall of Fame as one of the best US school and college baseball coaches of all time.

Mickey was a gifted player, but would constantly defy Bertman's authority by provoking him and showing a lack of respect. The coach took his revenge by dropping Mickey from the team at that critical moment when the scouts descended on the school. Some people would never get over a disappointment like that, but Mickey now realises it was his own fault and he was hurting himself with his bad attitude.

Mickey was a rebel in the way he dressed as well. Instead of the latest fashions worn by the cool kids around Miami, Mickey and his brother Joey favoured flamboyant, multi-coloured clothes. They would strut around like peacocks and you can only imagine the kind of names they were called by the local tough kids – name-calling that stopped when Joey hit one of the big-mouths with a baseball bat.

Mickey's eccentric fashion sense, which continues to this day, was raised to new outlandish levels after graduating from Miami Beach Senior High School in 1971. The favourite items in his wardrobe included platform shoes, satin trousers and women's blouses, some of which were borrowed from his mother. Completing his androgynous look was the way he wore his hair then, long and dyed blonde. He has no idea why he dressed like that, other than wanting to look as cool as his idol, Elvis Presley, and a feeling that he needed to fit in with his friends. Around this time, he had amassed a group of mates who all dressed in the same way and were equally directionless as to their future prospects.

Mickey left home as soon as he could and shared rooms with three of those pals at Miami's Wild West Hotel. Given their colourful dress sense and close friendship, many people, not surprisingly, thought they were gay. But Mickey and his mates were into women. In fact, there was nothing else on their minds, except for maybe acting cool and getting high. They would go to the 48th Street beach all morning, get tanned and chat up babes, sleep in the afternoon and hit the town at night, cruising around Miami, smoking joints and checking out the talent.

Mickey didn't get hooked on drugs in those beach bum days – and claims he hasn't since, despite the odd fling. Young Mickey's head was certainly clear enough to know he couldn't drift through life forever and needed to find a job. The problem was he couldn't find anything that interested him and subsequently drifted into a string of jobs – such as hotel car park attendant and restaurant dogsbody – that were short-lived because he would quit in frustration or get fired for having a bad attitude. He worked at a shooting range picking up bullet casings, but had to leave that job when he developed lead poisoning.

His attempt at being an electrician only lasted a day as he couldn't figure out how to work a machine he was asked to operate and didn't like that it kept giving him electric shocks. The future film star was a cinema usher for a while but lost that job when he got into a violent fight with another usher who had hit him over the head with his torch for a laugh.

Mickey was between jobs when Gary Cox, an old friend from his high school football team, approached him on the beach one day with a startling and life-altering proposition: 'Would you like to give acting a try?' Gary was now going to the University of Miami and directing a play there. One of the students had dropped out of it and he thought Mickey would make an ideal replacement in the now vacant role – that of a brawny tough guy. Mickey pointed out that he didn't go to the University of Miami, but his mate said that didn't matter as no one would notice.

Mickey hadn't shown any interest in acting back at Miami Beach Senior High School, unlike fellow pupils and future film stars Ellen Barkin and the aforementioned Andy Garcia, who were in lower years. But he had developed an interest in watching movies ever since his school English teacher, Zelda Glazer, showed him the first film he ever saw, *A Place in the Sun*. She screened the 1951 classic twice for her class of underachievers, which Mickey was in, and he remembers being fascinated by the performance of leading man Montgomery Clift. In 2009, that inspirational teacher's writer-director son, Mitch Glazer, would cast Mickey in the lead role of his forthcoming film, *Passion Plays*.

But Mickey's acting career might never have happened at all had the youngster not agreed, with little else to do, to check out that Miami play by attending a rehearsal.

The play was *Deathwatch* by Jean Genet and was about three prison inmates vying for leadership of their cell. Mickey got up on stage to read the role of Green Eyes, one of the prisoners, was immediately hooked on acting and agreed to do the show. He recalled, 'I really liked it. I don't think I was very good, you know, but it was like, hey, this is a great feeling. Whatever this is, this is neat.'

Mickey repeated the role at another local theatre, enjoyed himself even more, thought it was the most worthwhile thing he had done in quite some time and began to think acting could be the career for him. He reasoned, 'I pretty much lived in my mind anyway. I thought it would be real nice to be in a different place, to be somebody else, and I needed to do something else.' That was because his career options had come down to either acting or crime. His mates told him crime offered much greater guarantees of making money.

Mickey occasionally helped collect gambling debts by using a combination of menace and muscle and mixed with acquaintances who had graduated from petty crime to more serious activities. When Mickey went to hang out with them one day he found himself caught up in a gunfight as bullets suddenly whizzed by his head. He was smart enough to realise that sticking with this line of work could get him killed.

Acting seemed a much safer option and an opportunity presented itself when a theatre company in Chicago offered Mickey an apprenticeship, saying he could learn to act while making scenery. But he turned it down because he wasn't interested in building sets. He also eventually admitted to not even being able to hammer a nail in, so he went back to hanging out at the beach with his mates and wondering if there was an easier way to break into acting. Gary Cox, who cast him in *Deathwatch*, and went on to work as a waiter, had suggested he move to New York, which is where people went to become actors. It was certainly something to consider.

It was during a long talk about the future with one of his closest friends, Stoney Curtis – so named because he looked like Tony Curtis and loved getting stoned – that he came up with a firm plan. Mickey announced to his pal, 'I'm gonna move to New York and become an actor there.'

So that's what he did. He said goodbye to his colourful Miami mates – who presented him with a going away present of a baseball bat with which to ward off trouble-makers in New York – got on a plane for the first time in his life and, with $400 in his pocket which was borrowed from his sister Patti who was working at the local McDonald's, headed off to a hopefully bright future.

Looking for somewhere to stay in the Big Apple, he visited a number of addresses of people his grandmother used to know, only to find they had moved away or the buildings weren't even there any more. One place he did know existed was the world-famous Actors' Studio where he had heard that one of his favourite movie stars, Steve McQueen, had studied. So he picked up his suitcases, got in a cab and headed there. Mickey walked in, told the people inside that he had come to New York to be an actor but had little cash and no place to stay. They were nice enough to recommend some cheap hotels favoured by a lot of starving actors. He first tried the Albert and then the Earl before settling on a $38-a-week attic room at the Marlton on West 8th Street in Greenwich Village. That's where he would stay for the next few years.

Nervous about some of the bizarre characters he had seen in the hotel, Mickey took his baseball bat to bed with him every night. For the first month, he felt shy and alone. He knew nobody in the big city. Meanwhile, he had no money other than his accommodation expenses and would occasionally shoplift chocolate bars just to survive.

Things improved when a friend from Miami, Little Eddie, joined him at the Marlton. While Mickey had come to the Big Apple to be an actor, his friend's dream was to become a gangster. But with neither of those positions immediately available, they went out to look for other work together and both got jobs for a while working as attendants at a nearby car park.

Little Eddie was a 4ft 8in tall Cuban whose toughness had been almost legendary in Miami. He was such a fearless character that he once stood up in a cinema, where several other moviegoers were loudly talking during the film, and demanded that everyone should sit down and shut the fuck up. They did.

Little Eddie had used the McDonald's where Patti Rourke worked as his unofficial office. Mickey went storming in there one day to confront him after one of his other friends had been beaten up by the tiny tough guy. When he demanded to know why he'd done it, the Cuban coolly replied, 'Because he's a punk.' Mickey thought about it, realised his pal *was* a punk and decided he liked this weird little character. They became firm friends from that moment and Eddie always backed him up – once even coming to his rescue when four much bigger guys were beating up Mickey in the street.

The Cuban shared Mickey's bizarre fashion sense, too, and when they found themselves together in New York, the compadres from Miami broke out the old extravagant outfits. They made quite a sight walking along together through Greenwich Village in their glam rock gear, Little Eddie on the pavement and Mickey in the street to minimise the height difference whenever a girl went past. They had a fun time until Little Eddie moved away to Connecticut, much to Mickey's disappointment.

With his friend gone, Mickey would hit the town alone in his brightly-coloured clothes – and was soon fighting off advances from the neighbourhood homosexuals who presumed he was on the pull. He recalled in a later magazine interview, 'I was so fucking naïve walking around in my Cuban high-heeled shoes and my fucking stardust outfit that I didn't realise the cool boys on the corner were eyeballing me because they wanted to get down.'

Mickey thought he looked so cool and well dressed that one day he walked into the Ford Modelling Agency and asked for a job. He didn't get past the receptionist who looked at him as if he was nuts. But he really did need some kind of paying work if he was to survive in the big city. Thoughts of acting seemed to be forgotten as he bounced from one bizarre job to another. One of the oddest jobs he took was as an attack dog agitator, wearing a leather glove and encouraging Doberman Pinschers to sink their teeth into it as part of their guard dog training. 'That was one of my favourite ones,' he laughed, 'provoking a killer dog.'

He also worked for the brothels on 42nd Street, supervising the team of young men from Puerto Rico who handed out flyers on the street by making sure they did their job and didn't get beaten up or chased off by pimps. He then lost his job parking cars at a valet service because he kept crashing them due to his struggles backing the vehicles into tiny spaces.

All these low-paid jobs provided valuable life experience which would later be poured into his acting when he came to play characters with the odds stacked against them. Other actors who find work straight out of school for a teen series or soap opera never get that kind of insight.

But Mickey wasn't thinking back then about how lucky he was. Instead, he was just battling to scrape together enough money to pay for the fast food, crisps and chocolate bars which made up his diet. He knew nothing about nutrition back then and his teeth were rotting. He was also struggling to pay his bill to carry on staying at the rundown hotel where he was living. His grandmother would send him a few dollars each month to get by and the cash was vital to Mickey who would show up hours early at the Western Union money wiring office waiting to get his cheque.

It was a lonely time for Mickey with no close buddies around and no girlfriend. He was shy around the big city girls and didn't know how to talk to them. They certainly didn't come running like they did once he became famous. When he did hook up with a woman, they looked nothing like the glamorous models and actresses who would eventually choose to spend time with him.

His life back then was as much of a mess as his room at the Marlton – which looked as rough as some of the girls he took back to it. The chambermaids would sometimes refuse to clean the room because it was left in such squalor. With little cash, direction or prospects, it seemed a hopeless situation. But hope was about to walk into Mickey's life in the form of a kindly man who put him on the right track.

The great philosopher Albert Schweitzer once said, 'Sometimes our light goes out but is blown again into flame by an encounter with another human being. Each of us owes the deepest thanks to those who have rekindled this inner light.' Mickey owed his thanks to the night manager at the Marlton, Carl Montgomery, who befriended him and made him think seriously again about becoming an actor. Carl was a huge theatre buff who would talk with great enthusiasm to the young hotel guest about the plays and performers he had seen. He gave Mickey books and articles about acting and actors, plays by Shakespeare and Tennessee Williams, recommended old films for him to watch and really reignited his interest in acting. Mickey immersed himself in this fascinating new world.

Countless actors had passed through the hotel's doors over the years but Montgomery saw something in Mickey the others never had – star quality. He just didn't know if he had the dedication to make it.

Inspired by his chats with Carl, Mickey went back to the Actors' Studio, determined to try and win a place at the school where past students had included James Dean, Marlon Brando and Montgomery Clift – all actors Mickey had learned more about and become a huge fan of after the Marlton's night manager had widened his horizons. He learned that those legends, along with more recent students like Robert De Niro and Al Pacino, had studied the Stanislavski 'method' there, a style of performance originated by a Russian theatre revolutionary in which the actor puts his own life experience into the role to make it more real. That sounded good to Mickey but he wasn't going to be able just to walk into a place at this ultimate acting school as they received thousands of applications each year and only took on five students at a time.

Mickey realised he wasn't good enough yet to gain acceptance but, showing a dedication which had been missing from the rest of his life, he resolved to get the skills to make it in there some day soon and set about that ambition by signing up for private lessons with one of the Studio's top teachers, Sandra Seacat.

At first, she didn't know what to make of him. He was fascinating in his eccentricity but seemed so withdrawn and lacking in logic she even wondered if he might be a little retarded. But, using all her experience for bringing out talent, she gradually began to figure out Mickey and put him on the path to acting greatness. She found a way to channel all the frustration in his life into his performances. The breakthrough came when she gave him an acting exercise to do – pretending he was shining a pair of shoes.

Mickey later recalled, 'That was a job I hated because I'd had to do it for all my brothers when I was a kid. Seven pairs of shoes a day. As I was acting this, something just clicked. All the things that had been holding me back for years started coming out – the disappointment in sports, my sadness about never having got to know my father, everything fell into place. From that day on, it was like I'd finally stopped posing and become myself, a real person.'

Mickey added in a Q&A, 'I wanted to be the best actor I possibly could be. With the boxing it had never been 100 per cent but suddenly acting was. I had no social life. I studied like a monk. I would grab bums off the street to run lines with me at night.'

Seeing that level of commitment, drama coach Sandra Seacat felt it was time for Mickey to audition for a place at the Actors' Studio. It was preparing for that big test which forced Mickey to make a journey he might otherwise never have taken – a visit to his father.

His audition scene for the Studio was to be one from the Tennessee Williams play *Cat on a Hot Tin Roof* in which Brick discusses his drinking problem with his father, Big Daddy. While rehearsing it, he just wasn't able to make the father-and-son relationship convincing. Mickey talked it over with Seacat and she said he would continue to have a problem with that scene, and similar ones in the future, unless he got to know his own father. She advised her student to go and find his dad and talk to him.

Mickey was reluctant. He hadn't had any contact with Phil since his parents parted all those years before. But he was still holding on to that treasured photograph of his father in bodybuilding pose. Although Mickey wasn't keen to find out how time had changed his dad, his determination to improve his acting and win a place at the Actors' Studio was a powerful motivator and provided him with the courage to get on a bus to Schenectady.

The moment he arrived in town, Mickey noticed the White Castle diner where, as a child, he had enjoyed milkshakes with his father. He decided to go in and have one for old time's sake. But as he stepped inside, his attention was immediately drawn to a middle-aged man sitting alone. The man was wearing glasses and he certainly didn't look like a bodybuilder but it was unmistakably Phil Rourke. Mickey recognised him because of his hands – which looked just like his. He also had the same forehead and mouth. Mickey took a deep breath and went over to him.

He said, 'Are you Phil? I'm Mickey.' The man put his glasses halfway down his nose, looked at the young man standing in front of him, and replied, 'Is your mother here?'

His son shook his head. Phil looked disappointed for a

second, then he stared at Mickey, paused and said, 'I always knew you'd come to see me one day.'

Father and son then went to a place nearby to have dinner together and, fuelled by the many screwdrivers they nervously drank between them, the conversation eventually started to flow. Mickey kept saying things like, 'Dad, would you pass the salt?' and 'Dad, shall we get another drink?' so his father would know he still called him Dad.

In another emotional moment, he touched his dad's upper arm just like he used to do when he was a kid – but this time there was no muscle there, the skin was just soft. Mickey felt his stomach lurch at that moment. He couldn't believe this was the same powerfully-built man whose picture he had been carrying around for the past 17 years.

He told Phil about the Actors' Studio and was surprised to find his father also had an interest in theatre. Phil had once reviewed plays for an army newspaper when he was stationed in Germany as a young man. It upset Mickey that they had not been able to share this passion and had missed out on so many years together. Suddenly, he felt uncomfortable and got up to leave, but Phil pulled him back for one last drink – and did the same thing a couple more times.

Eventually, it was time for the last bus back to New York and, before Mickey got on board, Phil thrust $50 into his son's hand and said, 'Take it, you'll break my heart if you don't.' Then he suddenly embraced Mickey with a bear hug and started to cry.

During the bus journey back, young Mickey realised he felt less detached from his dad. But his thoughts drifted away from their emotional reunion and back to the *Cat on a Hot Tin Roof* scene he would have to perform for the audition panel the next morning. During the late-night bus ride and the eventual walk back to his room, Mickey wasn't wearing warm enough clothes and shivered all the way home as he tried to relate what he had just experienced in Schenectady to the acting task ahead.

The next day, as he nervously paced outside the audition room preparing for the make or break performance, he couldn't summon up those same feelings of awkwardness about his father. So, moments before he was due on stage, he rushed outside into the New York snow and took off his shirt to recreate the bitter cold he had felt the previous night. It served to put him in the same state of mind he had been feeling then – and Mickey was now ready to audition.

He blew away the panel with a performance of stunning realism – playing the scene as if he was talking to his own big daddy rather than the character. On the panel was Actors' Studio co-founder Elia Kazan, three-time Oscar-winning director of classic films like *On the Waterfront* and *East of Eden*, who said Mickey's piece was the best audition he had seen in 30 years.

It was a proud moment for Sandra Seacat, who continues to be a mentor to emerging actors and most recently discovered *Star Trek*'s new Captain Kirk, Chris Pine. The audition was a triumph for Mickey who was immediately offered that coveted place at the Actors' Studio and eagerly accepted.

But there was to be no happy ending to the story of him and his father. They did keep in touch after their reunion and Phil would write him letters every so often. But they were never to meet again for Phil passed away just a few years later aged just 49. 'He drank himself to death,' said Mickey.

Getting into the Actors' Studio, which he calls 'a sacred place', was a dream come true for Mickey – but you wouldn't know it from the way he behaved. He was shy, nervous and quiet around the students and staff. For his first two years there, he would just sit in a corner listening, too terrified to make a significant contribution in class.

Mickey would watch mesmerised as the likes of Christopher Walken, Harvey Keitel and Al Pacino – who were all making the step up from students to stars at the time – would stop by the Actors' Studio to hone their craft and seemingly have the ability to tap into different emotions at a moment's notice. He remembers being starstruck the first time he came face to face there with Keitel, whose work he had admired in the 1973 film *Mean Streets*. Keitel snapped his fingers at Mickey to get him to move out of his way. Mickey said of those stars, 'They had set the bar high and I wanted to be like them, to be that kind of actor.'

But it wasn't easy. Although opening up his emotions had landed him a place, he was too embarrassed to get up in front of the class and talk in public about his feelings. Yet he did enjoy the improvisation exercises in class and gradually started to flourish when hiding behind characters he would make up on the spot.

Tuition didn't come cheap and Mickey had to take another succession of short-lived jobs so he could continue paying for his classes. He was often fired and always broke but forever on the lookout for a shot at the big time. Unlike so many other acting students, he couldn't get a job as a waiter because his maths skills weren't good enough. For a time, he moved furniture in the same warehouse where Gene Hackman, Steve McQueen and Lee Marvin had all worked before getting their big breaks.

One job Mickey was able to hold down for a while was selling food from a cart at the side of Central Park close to the big casting agencies. He would sell pretzels and chestnuts in the winter and ice cream in the summer but, whatever the time of year, he always kept a pair on sunglasses in his pocket ready to whip out whenever someone who looked like a casting director walked past.

The tactic didn't lead to him getting any acting work. In fact, Mickey took five years of classes before he actively went looking for acting jobs. It was his mentor Sandra Seacat, who would continue to be a great support to him as he built a film career, who finally persuaded him to leave. She felt he was becoming part of the furniture at the Actors' Studio and told him so in no uncertain terms. Sandra yelled at him out in the street, 'Do you want to take classes for the rest of your life? Get out there and work.'

So Mickey tried to do just that. He looked for roles in off-Broadway experimental theatre and was hired, largely on the back of his impressive training. But he quit most shows during rehearsals as his old problems with authority figures returned and he clashed with the directors. If the play wasn't going the way he wanted, he would be gone. It seemed being part of a theatre company just wasn't for him.

Mickey got his first screen acting role in the 1976 short film, *Love in the Hamptons*. He had the lead role of Swede, a working-class young man in love with a waitress, and his dedication to authentic performances was already present. A moment before filming a scene in which his character wakes up in the morning, he threw a handful of sand in his eyes in order to create that gritty, eye-rub feeling people often have as soon as they get up. The five-day shoot went well and Mickey started to think his future lay in film rather than theatre.

But movies were mostly made in Los Angeles, whereas New York was a theatre town and, a couple of years later, Mickey decided to try his luck in films and so relocated to LA, aiming to become a star.

The bold ambition got off to a good start when he was signed up for representation by John Travolta's managers Bob LeMond and Lois Zetter and later got a good up-and-coming agent in Bernie Carneol, who worked around the clock trying to secure auditions for him. Now Mickey just needed to land some roles – but there was a problem which would be a constant barrier to his employment right then and for years to come.

While the Actors' Studio had given him the tools to do the job, it hadn't taught him the politics of the industry and how the business worked. There had been no classes in business skills. Consequently, he had no clue how to sell himself to casting agents. All the pleasantries of kissing ass and sucking up to these people for a role were a mystery to him. Mickey also had a particular acting technique where he would wait for the right feeling to descend on him before delivering his lines – but with dozens of other actors waiting to audition for the same part, casting agents wanted him to get on with it and couldn't hang around until he was emotionally ready to perform. As a result, Mickey kept blowing the opportunities with which he was presented. He went through 75 auditions before he got his first part.

The only steady work he did find during that time in LA was as a bouncer in a Hollywood Boulevard transvestite club called Danielle's. He was kept busy because the customers would come in high on angel dust, which gave them superhuman strength and led to them getting into violent fights. Mickey would try and break things up while raging trannies picked up steel napkin holders from the tables and threw them at him. One night, the other bouncer whacked one muscle-bound, high-as-a-kite transvestite over the head with a wooden club, only for the club to break in half and the customer kept advancing. After that incident, Mickey quit as a bouncer but kept on working there in the slightly safer job as a waiter. He couldn't turn his back on Danielle's entirely because he would get the odd TV or film acting job here and there but never the kind of big-paying major role or regular work which would allow him to pursue acting full time.

But the breakthrough opportunity finally came when he went along on his lunch break from the transvestite club to audition for a small but flashy part as a streetwise arsonist alongside William Hurt in the 1981 thriller movie *Body Heat*. This time, Mickey greatly impressed the casting agents with his audition and was offered the part – a role which would finally put him on the Hollywood map.

But instead of saying 'Thanks very much' and gratefully grabbing the job with both hands, Mickey's stubborn streak returned and he insisted the moviemakers should improve their financial offer to him or he wouldn't take the role. The offer was $500 a day for two days' work, but

Mickey, despite being a virtual nobody, demanded $1,000 a day.

His agent, Bernie Carneol, couldn't believe it and thought Mickey had lost his mind. In near despair, he told him, 'But Mickey, you work in a transvestite club . . . take the offer!'

Showing an unwillingness to compromise – which would be the hallmark of his personality for years to come – Mickey held out for the extra $500 a day he felt he was worth. And he got it.

It wasn't so much that he was business savvy, Mickey just wanted everything done on his own terms as usual. This 'my way or the highway' approach on *Body Heat* became a feature of his future dealings with film bosses.

Mickey made the absolute most of his opportunity in *Body Heat*, playing the part to perfection with a mix of swagger and quiet confidence. His twitchy, spellbinding performance caught the eye of Hollywood's top casting directors. He was now on his way to the Hollywood dream.

Little did he know then, it would soon turn into a nightmare.

2

A Life on Screen – Part I

C aked in make-up, smeared with thick lipstick, wearing a red bra and various other items of women's clothing while tottering along on powder-blue ladies' shoes, Mickey Rourke boarded a plane from LA to Vancouver. It was all part of his method acting approach to playing a transvestite in the 2000 movie *Animal Factory*.

Instead of waiting to get changed on the set in Canada, Mickey decided to live the role for real by donning drag for the plane journey over to the filming location. The very convincing outfit had been painstakingly put together after ten days' shopping at flamboyant LA boutiques like Trashy Lingerie. He was wearing such long, fake fingernails that he struggled to pull his flight ticket out of his pocket at the boarding gate. A little boy behind him was watching in fascination. Mickey smiled down at him but the strangely dressed star didn't have in his two front teeth – which are false as a legacy of his boxing days – and the poor lad was so scared he ran and hid behind his mother's skirt.

On the flight itself, Mickey took his seat and noticed the other passengers staring at him. Unsettled by their attention, he developed a blotchy rash. When the flight attendant first came down the aisle asking passengers, 'Would you like a drink, sir?' or 'Would you like a drink, ma'am?' she got to Mickey, looked unsure, dispensed with both 'sir' and 'ma'am' and enquired, 'Can I get you anything?'

When he got to the set in drag and said hello to the director, Steve Buscemi, Steve didn't recognise him at first. Eventually, the star had to say, 'It's me, Mickey!' Buscemi looked aghast and replied, 'Jesus Christ!'

But Mickey was brilliant in the film – just one of many great performances he has given over the past 30 years.

■　■　■

It's hardly surprising, in view of Mickey Rourke's often disappointing box-office returns, that he should have been involved in Steven Spielberg's only massive flop. Mickey's first movie credit – he's actually listed 68th in the cast list – comes as Private Reese in *1941* (1979), an absurd wartime farce about Californians lapsing into a panic at the prospect of a Japanese invasion. Spielberg had intended it as a 'stupidly outrageous celebration of paranoia'. Well, he got the stupid part right. Audiences quite rightly ignored the daft movie, which starred John Belushi and Dan Aykroyd.

The only slight consolation for Mickey was that the film's failure wasn't his fault. He hung around the set for ten weeks but didn't even get an appearance in the final cut for his trouble. Mickey waited for his part to materialise, but it never did – a rough introduction to the big time.

But he did make a fleeting appearance in *Fade to Black* (1980), a weird little horror movie starring Dennis Christopher as a strange young man whose obsession with movies leads him to dress up as film stars and carry out a killing spree. Mickey was 11th on the cast list this time in the role of Richie, but the movie failed to make any kind of impact.

He had high hopes for his next film, though, and with big talent involved and big money behind it, what could possibly go wrong? Plenty, as it turned out. The film was *Heaven's Gate* (1980), one of the biggest commercial and creative disasters of all time. A rambling Western about cattlemen in old Wyoming, *Heaven's Gate* drags on for a bottom-numbing 219 minutes with nothing much happening.

Mickey was thrilled to be working with director Michael Cimino and co-star Christopher Walken who, just a month before filming started, had both won Oscars for *The Deer Hunter* – a favourite of Mickey's and the only film he has watched more than three times. But his excitement got the better of him at first. Nerves took hold as he prepared to shoot a scene with Walken, an old acquaintance and idol of his from The Actors' Studio, and when Cimino called 'Action!', Mickey froze, completely unable to say his lines.

Cimino's reaction was to take Mickey aside, call him a 'dumb son of a bitch' and hit him with his hat. Mickey actually responded well to that approach, was fine from that point on and had a lot of respect for Cimino.

He ended up bonding well with Walken, who had one of the lead roles as a hired gun while Mickey had a tiny part as one of his gun-toting sidekicks, Nick Ray (33rd in the credits this time).

Despite getting off to a bad start, he gradually also made a good impression on director Michael Cimino, and learned a lot about the movie-making process during the 12 weeks he was on the set.

Cimino went way over budget and schedule, taking eight months to shoot the débâcle. After five days on set, he was already four days behind schedule. He was determined that the film should be his unique vision and, to ensure that happened, he posted an armed security guard outside the editing room to keep executives from the film studio, United Artists, away.

Its spectacular failure at the box office bankrupted United Artists, and led to a Hollywood re-think on big-budget epics. The movie cost $36 million and made back just $1 million at US cinemas. Critics found the story totally incoherent and were particularly savage about Cimino, whose career struggled to recover from the setback.

Another black mark against the movie was the scale of animal abuse that took place during production. At least four animals died on set, including chickens which were decapitated, in a film which featured horse torture and cockfights. The outcry prompted new rules in Hollywood, with the American Humane Society brought in afterwards to monitor the use and treatment of animals in all US films and TV shows.

Mickey only makes a blink-and-you'll-miss-him appearance in the final cut of *Heaven's Gate* but the experience at least gave him time to get to know Walken and Cimino, both of whom he would go on to work with in future and in more entertaining films.

Mickey then landed his first notable film role in steamy thriller *Body Heat* (1981) playing a charismatic criminal in just a couple of scenes but stealing the movie from its stars, William Hurt and Kathleen Turner. Director Lawrence Kasdan was looking for a young Robert De Niro and, when

Mickey read for the role, it was as though the heir to that great actor had suddenly emerged.

Body Heat sees Hurt's character, a lawyer, plotting to kill his lover's husband and going to see a client, soft-spoken arsonist Teddy Lewis, for advice on how to do the deed. When Mickey, as Lewis, describes how to set a fire, he conveys everything through a quiet stillness, leaning in close, staring thoughtfully and lowering his voice as he warns his lawyer to reconsider what he's doing. It was the first of many bad boys with a conscience he would play down the years. Mickey's now familiar mannerisms and scorching talent were all on show here and the film also marked the start of his long career of saying 'fuck' on screen.

Many critics praised his work in their reviews of *Body Heat* and Hollywood sat up and took notice of the newcomer. The James Dean comparisons started here but Mickey, with his halting delivery of lines, was more of a rebel with a pause.

Now Mickey could quit his job at the transvestite club and sift through the film offers that started to come in as leading moviemakers clamoured to work with him. Lawrence Kasdan offered Mickey a role in his next film, *The Big Chill*, but was turned down as the actor didn't want to do a film about 'a whole bunch of yuppies'. Instead, Mickey signed up for comedy drama *Diner* (1982) for which writer-director Barry Levinson assembled a cast of unknowns with the potential to become big stars.

Levinson clearly knew what he was doing because his other casting choices included Kevin Bacon and Steve Guttenberg, as well as Ellen Barkin, who had gone to the same school as Mickey but had not known him back then.

Mickey was easily the best of the bunch, showing a mix of toughness and vulnerability as girl-chasing hairdresser Boogie Sheftell.

Set in 1959, the movie follows a group of longtime friends who meet up at a Baltimore diner to discuss girls, gambling and life in general, courtesy of some sharp, funny dialogue from Levinson, who was to go on to direct *Good Morning Vietnam* and *Rain Man*. The Baltimore diner used in the film was a real one, not a set, but is no longer in business, having re-opened 20 years later as a job training centre for disadvantaged youths. Levinson based the script on the kind of mates he had hung out with while growing up. They certainly weren't the kind Mickey had grown up around – he would have found them all too boring for his taste. But his role as Boogie was a good part and Mickey really shone in his first substantial film appearance, showcasing a sweet smile and a cheeky charm as the smooth-talking skirt-chaser.

The movie is best remembered for the scene in which Boogie bets his pals that he can get a beautiful blonde to touch his 'pecker' on their first date at a cinema. He wins the bet by sticking it through the bottom of the popcorn box on his lap and giving her the shock of her life when she reaches in to grab a handful. Mickey's real acting genius, though, comes in the next scene where he convinces the startled bimbo to forgive him by spinning her a tall tale that it was all an innocent accident caused by his excitement at sitting next to her getting the better of him.

While his acting instincts were spot on, the same couldn't be said for his make-up choices. On *Diner*, Mickey insisted on doing his own eye make-up – because Christopher

Walken had once told him that's what he always did. So Mickey pulled out his own make-up kit and set to work on the set – the odd results can be seen in various scenes. Eventually, the director of photography pulled him aside one day and told him to let the professionals do it instead, saying, 'Listen, we're not doing *Dracula*.'

As good as he was in the film, Mickey wasn't especially wild at the time about *Diner* or any of his colleagues. But he was most enthusiastic to be teaming up with Nicolas Roeg, a director he greatly admired, on his next film, *Eureka* (1983). Mickey had always gone to Roeg films, such as *Don't Look Now* and *The Man Who Fell to Earth*, on the first day they came out. So he jumped at the opportunity to work on the moviemaker's latest complex drama, especially as part of the filming was to be done in Jamaica, which sounded like a great place to combine business with pleasure.

Eureka is the story of a troubled billionaire, played by Gene Hackman, battling mobsters who want to open a casino on the Caribbean island he owns. Mickey, in thick-rimmed glasses and with slicked-back hair, plays Aurelio D'Amato, a lawyer working for a Mafia boss, who has been sent round to make the tycoon an offer he can't refuse – or else. Mickey didn't care for the part at all but did enjoy being around Roeg and was amused when the director would anger some of the other actors on the film by telling them how to say their lines properly. In the end, few people ended up seeing *Eureka*, which opened in only a handful of cinemas around the world before quickly disappearing.

Mickey then really found a role to sink his teeth into with *Rumble Fish* (1983), Francis Ford Coppola's visually stunning adaptation of the Susie Hinton novel about troubled youths in Tulsa. As a huge fan of the director's masterpiece *The Godfather*, Mickey had eagerly auditioned for a role in Coppola's previous film, *The Outsiders*, and while he hadn't been right for that one – he was too old for a film about teenage gangs – the director was hugely impressed with the newcomer and decided to cast him as the enigmatic older brother, Motorcycle Boy, in his next picture.

Mickey was so grateful and determined to please Coppola that he resolved to give the performance everything he had. His dedication to certain roles first showed itself on this film. To prepare for playing such a weird character, Mickey dyed his hair red and wore bright green contact lenses – even though the movie was shot in black and white. What impressed Coppola more was the subtle way Mickey managed to make his character so charismatic despite having few lines. It was all due to an acting technique he had never witnessed before or since.

Each day, Mickey would come to him with an object, such as a ring, a stone or some other amulet, show it to the director and then put it in his pocket. For the rest of the day while filming scenes, he would focus his thoughts on the object in his pocket rather than the lines he was saying or what was happening in the scene. That approach most likely came from reading some advice about acting for the screen once given by Marlon Brando who had said, 'You can't care or they'll see it in your face.' In other words, if the actor is concentrating on something else rather than the action in the scene then the performance will feel more natural because, in real life, people are so often doing one thing while thinking about something else.

Mickey's part gave him plenty to think about – and a lot to relate to as Motorcycle Boy has an alcoholic father, resents his mother for moving away when he was very young and has a younger brother he adores. While the film was being made in Tulsa, Mickey received the devastating news that his brother was diagnosed with cancer – the first of many bouts Joey would have with the disease.

To further personalise the performance, the photograph Mickey's character uses as a bookmark – which is supposed to show Motorcycle Boy as a toddler with a protective arm around his brother when he was a baby – was actually an old photo of Mickey and Joey Rourke. It can be seen in close-up at one point in the movie.

The bond of brothers was what appealed most to Francis Ford Coppola about the story. He had always looked up to his own dapper and handsome older brother, August – to whom the film is dedicated. *Rumble Fish* marks the movie acting début of August's son, Nicolas Cage – or Nicolas Coppola as he was then credited – who plays tough guy Smoky and wears one of his dad's old jackets in the film.

Aside from Cage, the movie featured several other young cast members who would go on to big things, like Diane Lane, Larry Fishburne and, in the role of Motorcycle Boy's younger brother Rusty James, Matt Dillon. But it's Mickey who stands out from the pack – not just for his world-weary performance but for his look, too. Instead of wearing the traditional moody movie biker outfit of black leather, his character dresses in a very different, more sophisticated way – a look Coppola says was inspired by the French philosopher Albert Camus. He had given Mickey some Camus novels and a biography of Napoleon to help him prepare for the role.

It is because Motorcycle Boy is colour-blind that the movie is almost entirely shot in black and white. The only colour in the film is provided by the two exotic fish which give the move its title. If you put two Rumble Fish – or Siamese Fighting Fish – in the same tank they will fight until one kills the other. Mickey's character is killed at the end – the first of many times he would die in the closing moments of movies – after he and his brother free the fish and all the other pets from a pet shop.

Coppola ranks *Rumble Fish* as one of the best films he has ever made – but it became, along with musical *One from the Heart*, one of the least financially successful movies of his whole career.

The first time Mickey remembers being disenchanted with the film business was when *Rumble Fish* was not well received on release. As Mickey had found with *Heaven's Gate*, and earlier with *1941*, a much-lauded director was now being laughed at for making a risky project. But Mickey wasn't amused.

His mood won't have been lightened by the largely negative reviews for his own performance in the film which was such a trademark display of method acting that several critics suggested the movie would have been more appropriately called 'Mumble Fish'.

But his spirits were lifted by his next film, *The Pope of Greenwich Village* (1984), which provided Mickey with the most fun he has ever had on a movie. It was the first of three films in a row he was to make that were set in New York and he was thrilled to be back on the streets of his favourite city. But the biggest thrill came from co-starring with Eric Roberts, whom he calls 'the best actor I ever worked with'.

Few actors can steal scenes from Mickey Rourke but Roberts at least matches him all the way in this thoroughly entertaining tale of two cousins who steal a safe full of Mob money and get into big trouble with both the cops and the Mafia.

The film was originally due to star acting greats Al Pacino and Robert De Niro, but Mickey and Roberts proved more than able replacements. Eric's role was as wayward cousin Paulie while Mickey starred as the smarter, more sophisticated cousin, Charlie Moran, and he spent $10,000 of his own money buying elegant clothes for his sharply dressed character to wear in the film. He also prepared for the part by spending three months before filming hanging out in the dive bars of Greenwich Village getting to meet the patrons, Mob guys and local characters. But his dedication to duty would best be shown once the cameras started rolling.

One scene called for Mickey to have a blazing row with his on-screen girlfriend, played by Daryl Hannah, which ended with her punching him hard in the face. Daryl connected so well that she knocked a cap off one of Mickey's teeth. Mickey didn't mind but he was glad when director Stuart Rosenberg, who had previously made *Cool Hand Luke* and *The Amityville Horror*, chose not to ask for a second take.

Pope wasn't a hit but won good reviews and has many fans. Johnny Depp loves the movie and calls it 'perfect cinema'. A big reason the movie still holds up well today is the interplay between Mickey and Roberts. In February 2009, when he was named Best Actor for *The Wrestler* at the Independent Spirit Awards, Mickey used his acceptance speech to pay tribute to his *Pope of Greenwich Village* co-star and urged the moviemakers present to give Eric Roberts a second shot at stardom, just like he had been given.

Mickey's next shot at acting greatness was to come with his biggest role to date, the lead in crime thriller *Year of the Dragon* (1985). He played crusading cop Stanley White, bravely waging a one-man war against the Chinese Mafia in New York. The movie marked Michael Cimino's return to directing after the *Heaven's Gate* fiasco and he and Mickey got to work with a well-crafted script by Oliver Stone which blurred the lines of good and evil.

Crowds flocked to cinemas when the movie opened in America in the late summer of 1985 but they weren't fighting to get in – instead, they were protesting against its showing. The film was slammed by politicians and citizens for alleged racism and violence in its depiction of New York's Chinese community. The critics slaughtered the film, too – much to Mickey's dismay. He felt the poor reviews were nothing to do with the movie but, instead, were a backlash against Michael Cimino who had become a punch bag for the press since *Heaven's Gate*.

Year of the Dragon was a commercial and critical failure but Mickey found that hard to take at the time, saying, 'The critics who destroyed that picture are the scum of the earth. May they burn in hell – and you can put that down.' He was so distraught that he seriously considered quitting the movie business there and then and launching a new career by opening a motorbike shop. It sounded more appealing than exposing himself to more of the aggravation. Mickey felt especially hurt as he had put so much work into the performance, researching the role by spending three months shadowing a real cop called Stanley White – whom his character is named after in thanks – and going out on homicide calls with him.

Mickey had also worked hard on developing a completely different look in that film, having dyed his hair grey as his character was supposed to be much older than him. But his younger and sexier look in his next film would make him one of the most desired men on the planet. Mickey lost weight, got in shape and had a neat haircut for the erotic drama *9½ Weeks* (1986), the movie that really put him on the map. The screenplay was based on a book of the same name, supposedly a memoir of her own erotic experiences by New Yorker Elizabeth McNeil, which, it later emerged, was the pen-name of a half-Swedish, half-French woman called Ingebord Day.

Mickey played rich, mysterious and dangerous stockbroker John who seduces up-for-it art gallery assistant Elizabeth, played by Kim Basinger, into a series of kinky sex games. From the moment they first meet, she is putty in his hands. The guilty pleasure of a film is full of steamy scenes like their quickie in the clock tower, her crawling across the floor picking up money and, most memorably, the food orgy. In that scene, John orders Elizabeth to close her eyes and slide down to the kitchen floor in front of his open refrigerator. He then tantalizes her tongue with food from the fridge such as strawberries, jelly, peppers, pasta, and then adds Vicks cough syrup and milk.

Hundreds of actresses had been seen for the role of Elizabeth, who falls under John's erotic spell, before the moviemakers settled on relative newcomer Basinger, who had broken into movies three years earlier as the Bond girl Domino in Sean Connery's *Never Say Never Again*. The stunning blonde was considered to have the perfect look and personality for the part.

Although Mickey and Kim generate real erotic heat on screen – so much so that they were voted the sexiest movie couple ever in a 2008 *Moviefone* survey – their relationship was colder off camera. She didn't like his smoking habit and called him 'the human ashtray'. Neither was she amused by Mickey's habit of blasting his favourite Billy Idol song, 'Rebel Yell', at full volume on set right before takes in order to help him get into character.

But Basinger and Mickey never really got to know each other – and that was a deliberate choice. Director Adrian Lynne didn't want them to meet before filming in order that they would be more convincing when meeting as strangers in the movie. In fact, the first time Mickey laid eyes on Basinger was just before filming the scene in the Chinese butcher's shop where their characters encounter each other for the first time. They kept their distance from each other during the rest of filming, too, and, despite being so intimate on screen, had virtually no relationship off camera. It would be 23 years before they would meet again.

To research his financial trader role, Mickey went to Wall Street and the New York Stock Exchange – and hated every minute of his visit. He reflected he would rather dig ditches than work there. Mickey thought long and hard about his own look in the film and went out and bought $12,000 worth of suits he thought his character would wear in the movie.

Adrian Lyne took one look at them and said, 'Mate, they're all wrong.' He said they were too flashy for a stockbroker and more appropriate to the character he had played in *The Pope of Greenwich Village*. Instead of taking them back to the shop, Mickey kept them all for himself, wearing instead the Brooks Brothers suits the costume department came up with for the film. He wanted to have spiky hair in the film like Billy Idol, but Lyne wanted it flatter and there were regular disputes because whenever the on-set hairdresser styled his hair for scenes, Mickey would run off to the bathroom and spike it up in front of the mirror and return with his newly primped hair ready for filming.

Director Lyne, as he had proved with his earlier movie *Flashdance*, has a great visual style and the movie had a terrific, atmospheric look, like one of the finest 1980s pop videos. In one scene, it was atmospheric to the detriment of Mickey's health. So much blue smoke was pumped around the chic boutique in the scene where John buys Elizabeth a dress that Mickey developed a bronchial problem and was off sick for two days.

Mickey liked the director, but didn't feel the finished movie went far enough, thinking the sado-masochism angle could have been pushed much further. Basinger didn't share his opinion but Mickey had hoped to be able to contribute to an all-out erotic masterpiece, bolder than anything in Brando's *Last Tango in Paris*, and didn't like the compromises in the final cut.

But plenty of people were perfectly happy with 9½ *Weeks* and Mickey became an international star on the film's release. And his growing fan base eagerly awaited their idol's next move.

But Mickey was prepared to keep them waiting. Hurt by

the critical slaying of *Year of the Dragon* and the safe editing of 9½ *Weeks*, he was disillusioned with the business, in no rush to get back in front of the cameras and was prepared to sit it out until a masterpiece came his way. He took a year off, spending lots of money, giving lots away and very quickly the cash started to run out. Mickey realised he had to get back to work – and needed to grab the best script available.

Mickey Rourke was one of four actors under consideration for the lead role in supernatural thriller *Angel Heart* (1987). But when he met with director Alan Parker in LA to discuss the film, he managed to convince him that only he could play the part and so there was no point talking to the other contenders. Parker knew about Mickey's growing reputation for not showing up for work on time and being difficult with directors, so he hired him on the condition that his leading man acted with total professionalism.

While Mickey knew that the role of private detective Harry Angel was a good one, the greater motivation for wanting the job was a desire to keep his house. Mickey had been spending money like crazy and realised that the large *Angel Heart* pay cheque would enable him to keep up his $25,000-a-month mortgage payments and pay off various other bills.

Rich in dark atmosphere, gorgeously shot and brilliantly acted by Mickey, *Angel Heart* is arguably Mickey's best film – at least until *The Wrestler* came along two decades later.

Set in 1955, it sees his private-eye character hired by a sinister man called Louis Cyphre (the clue is in the name) to track down a former client named Johnny Favorite who owes him something but has mysteriously disappeared. Harry's manhunt leads from New York to New Orleans, past a trail of dead bodies, into a romance with a young voodoo princess called Epiphany Proudfoot and ends with a creepy and shocking twist.

Mickey had a series of ideas for his character, including giving him a giant fake nose, jet-black hair and a limp – each of which Parker rejected.

The best scenes in the film are the ones between Mickey and Robert De Niro, who played Louis Cyphre – a chilling role that almost went instead to Marlon Brando. Mickey relished the opportunity to share the screen with one of the true acting greats and someone he respected hugely. He learned a lot from seeing just how focused and disciplined De Niro was – two qualities Mickey had struggled with ever since his amateur boxing days. He was determined to show he had great skills, too, and seeing them square off is almost like watching two heavyweight boxing legends battling for supremacy. One acting trick he used to create the right level of fear to film an encounter with his co-star's creepy character was for Mickey to imagine himself being eight years old again and having to face his terrifying stepfather. And to help him feel the tension while filming their climactic scene, Mickey clutched an ice cube in his fist. By the time it was completed, there was a puddle next to his feet. Mickey still keeps on his wall at home a photo he had taken on the set with De Niro.

Parker loved Mickey's work with De Niro, but the director had to rein him in during his scene with Charlotte Rampling, in the role of Margaret Krusemark. She was word perfect on every take but Mickey would go off script and improvise new lines each time in a bid to find a fresh way to play the scene. Parker felt the best way to do the scene was by delivering the words that were written and firmly told his star to stick to the script. The director would eventually call Mickey 'a nightmare' to work with because of his unpredictability, but he admired his acting genius at the same time.

In the scene near the end of the film when Harry Angel confronts Ethan Krusemark and reacts violently when much of the terrible truth is explained to him, Mickey was, accidentally, a little too violent. It called for him to clamp ice tongs to the side of the head of actor Stocker Fontelieu, who was playing Krusemark, but it turned out the rusty tongs were still quite sharp and blood started trickling from Stocker's temples. Alan Parker suddenly remembered he hadn't asked for any theatrical blood and quickly called cut so the actor could get attention. They abandoned the scene immediately and picked it up again a couple of days later, by which time the ice tongs had been blunted before they were handed over to Mickey.

On its release, the film became best known for its controversial sex scene between Mickey's character and Epiphany Proudfoot, played by Lisa Bonet, who at the time was starring in American TV's most successful and most wholesome sitcom, *The Cosby Show*. Seeing her romp naked amid a shower of blood with Mickey's character, who it is later revealed is her father, was almost too much for the US ratings board and Mickey had to make a personal plea, along with Alan Parker, in front of the censors before the film – with a crucial few seconds cut from bloody bonk scene – was eventually cleared for release in the States.

Angel Heart served to make Mickey appear even more iconic and cool. *9½ Weeks* director Adrian Lyne said that if

Mickey had died after *Angel Heart*, he would have instantly become as famous as James Dean.

In this period, all of Hollywood's top scripts were coming his way but Mickey, who had by now developed an attitude problem, refused to listen to advice or do what he was told. He turned down the major movies and, instead, made his own vanity projects. His next roles would be an IRA gunman in *A Prayer for the Dying*, a shambling alcoholic in *Barfly*, a washed-up boxer in a film he wrote himself, *Homeboy*, a disfigured criminal in *Johnny Handsome* and even St Francis of Assisi in *Francesco*. All the films flopped and served to derail Mickey's promising career.

Mickey took half his usual salary to star as a disillusioned IRA terrorist in the low-budget thriller *A Prayer for the Dying* (1987) because he believed in the project and thought it would be a serious examination of the Irish Troubles. But he soon learned that producer Samuel Goldwyn Jr had a different vision for the film and saw it as a conventional action movie with plenty of gunfire and killings.

The pair clashed repeatedly with Goldwyn telling Mickey that his Northern Irish accent was too thick and hard to understand – that hurt Mickey who had worked for four months with dialogue coach Brendan Gunn to come up with a speaking voice so convincing that you would believe he had been born in a field of shamrocks. On day one of filming, he had the line, 'If you're dead, does it matter?' With his accent, it sounded like, 'If yer da'ed, does it motter?' One of Goldwyn's representatives came over to ask why he had to say it like that – and the problems only got worse from that point. The producer also felt that

Mickey's performance could be more upbeat and less lethargic and that he would like his character to shoot more people.

Mickey's frustration and anger with the way the film was going was plain to see when Jack Higgins – author of the novel on which the movie was based – asked him for an autograph for his then 16-year-old daughter, Hannah, and Mickey wrote: 'To Hannah – we all know it's a pile of crap, Mickey.'

The whole shoot was a stressful experience for the actor who only got through it by listening to relaxation tapes he had flown over from California. Nevertheless, he managed to turn in a fine performance as gunman Martin Fallon who wants out of the killing business but is pursued for his services by a ruthless gangster, played by Alan Bates, and an IRA associate, played by Liam Neeson. Bob Hoskins is terrific, too, as a priest trying to make the terrorist do the right thing. Mickey also praised the performance of Sammi Davis, who plays his love interest, but still felt she was too young to do love scenes with him because, although 22 at the time, she looked creepily younger.

When he saw the final cut of the movie, Mickey's world imploded. He had set out to make a sensitive portrayal of the situation in Northern Ireland but felt the film had been turned into a standard sex and shoot-'em-up thriller.

A Prayer for the Dying, directed by crime film veteran Mike Hodges, quickly died at the box office but the controversy surrounding the subject matter and the star would rage on for a long time. Mickey fell into a depression for months afterwards at the way he felt his vision for the movie had been betrayed and he lost trust in people.

Mickey needed a lot of persuading to take on his next role as an alcoholic in *Barfly* (1987), especially as so many of his relatives had died from the demon drink. His father, grandfather, great-grandfather and uncles all perished after booze addictions. So the last thing he wanted to do was glorify a drunk on screen. But he was in a dark place mentally at the time and the darkness of the script appealed to him.

Barfly was based on the life of hard-drinking writer and poet Charles Bukowski, who wrote the film's screenplay. Mickey plays the very similar Henry Chinaski, a drunk who cruises seedy Los Angeles bars in an alcoholic haze and seems to enjoy frequently getting beaten up in bar brawls. But when a literary editor recognises his writing talent, Henry's freewheeling lifestyle is suddenly under threat.

Mickey had never heard of Bukowski before filming but read a couple of his books, met the writer as preparation and got to like him – as did his brother Joey who became a drinking partner of the writer. Bukowski was a real character on set, drinking beer from early in the morning and trying to persuade Mickey to have one. But even though he was playing an alcoholic, Mickey stuck to ginseng, vitamins and protein shakes during filming of the movie.

He also enjoyed working with colourful co-star Faye Dunaway – who would often be on the phone with her shrink for an hour before filming her first scene of the day – but didn't think much of the movie's director, Barbet Shroeder, whom he has since called 'a prick' and 'a baby' and an 'asshole'.

Shroeder certainly went to extremes in order to get the movie made. The company which had been developing the film, Cannon, was all set to cancel it for financial reasons until the eccentric director showed up at the office of their president Menahem Golan with an electric saw. He threatened to cut his own finger off there and then if the movie wasn't given an immediate go ahead. To show he was serious, he pulled out a syringe of the painkiller Novocain and injected it into his little finger. He then said he would continue cutting off parts of his body until *Barfly* got the green light. Golan told him to go to hell. Then Shroeder turned on the saw. Whether it was a bluff or not, it worked and *Barfly* went into production soon afterwards.

Mickey created one of his iconic characters in this film and few who saw it would forget the image of him shuffling down the more tattered streets of LA, sloppily dressed, unshaven and out of it.

A couple of years after the movie came out, Charles Bukowski wrote a novel called *Hollywood* which was a fictional account of his experiences during production of *Barfly* and it is clear to see who might have been the inspiration for the character of Jack Bledsoe, the eccentric lead actor who is surrounded by an entourage of street urchins and pseudo gangsters.

Mickey would continue to be associated with Bukowski even up to the writer's death. In its obituary of the poet in 1994, the *New York Post* used a photo of Mickey as Henry Chinaski in the film instead of a picture of Bukowski himself.

Barfly was a positive experience for Mickey overall and made him feel a bit better about the world after losing his way following *A Prayer for the Dying*. His spirits were about to be lifted even further when he got the go-ahead to star in a movie he had long dreamed of making. *Homeboy* (1988) was a true passion project for Mickey, who wrote the script himself under the pen name of Eddie Cook. The history of that name lay in it being the false one he had once given to the cops after stealing some chocolate when he was a kid. Years later, it was still a name he was happy to hide his true identity behind.

The story of a brain-damaged boxer drifting from fight to fight long after he should have retired from the sport, *Homeboy* was inspired by the path Mickey may have taken in life if he hadn't stepped away from boxing when he did.

It saw his character, soft-spoken cowboy Johnny Walker – based on a troubled fighter who used to box in the same Miami gym as Mickey all those years ago – risking his life in the ring for one last shot at big winnings. His unscrupulous manager, Wesley Pendegrass, who hides the extent of his medical condition from him, is played by Christopher Walken. The slow-paced film comes alive when they are on screen together, especially in the scene where Wesley tells the fighter his theory about why dinosaurs became extinct. That scene had its beginnings nine years earlier when Mickey and Walken were having dinner at the Outlaw Inn in Kalispell, Montana, after a day's filming on *Heaven's Gate*. Walken outlined his theory about what happened to the dinosaurs – that they grew wings and flew away to another planet. That conversation with one of his idols stayed in Mickey's mind and when he wrote *Homeboy* and cast Walken in the film, he deliberately gave Christopher's character a bizarre speech about dinosaurs turning into birds.

Mickey's love interest in the film, Ruby, was played by his wife, Debra Feuer, from whom he was estranged at the time. Their characters share a sweet, tender and ultimately doomed romance but Mickey and Debra display a curious lack of chemistry on screen. Mickey had written the role with Feuer in mind and the pair had a good working relationship, despite the fact that their marriage was nearing its end.

As close as he was to the material, Mickey chose not to direct *Homeboy*. It was originally his intention to do so, and he spent a couple of weekends shooting some test footage. But when Mickey saw it he realised he wasn't technically knowledgeable enough to create the look he wanted. So he brought in *Angel Heart*'s cinematographer Michael Seresin to direct the movie. He gave the film a terrific look, although the first-time director wasn't quite as successful with the pacing as the story drags in places.

Homeboy features cameos from some of boxing's most beloved figures, including ring announcer Michael Buffer, legendary trainer Bobby Slayton and ex-champ Iran Barkley. The film's memorable music was written and performed by Eric Clapton.

While *Homeboy* wasn't a commercial hit, the movie certainly has its moments and everyone involved could be proud of their efforts. Mickey followed it with another low-budget independent film but one that offered a very different role than fans had seen from him before or since – and a performance of which he was very proud.

Francesco (1989) saw him play St Francis of Assisi. Given his off-screen reputation as something of a sinner, it was a surprise to see Mickey cast to play a saint. But that was largely what had drawn him to the project in the first place. Mickey had been raised in the Catholic faith and is still a regular churchgoer who says his prayers every day. Some of his earliest memories are of going to church with his father and eating doughnuts and drinking milk with him afterwards. When his mother broke up with her husband and moved away to Miami with the kids, she joined the Episcopal Church and took Mickey along. But when he was 17 and facing an uncertain future, Mickey decided to switch back to Catholicism and has stuck with his faith ever since.

He knew about several saints but wasn't too familiar with St Francis until he read up on him as research for *Francesco*. When he learned Francis had been a pampered playboy who lived life in the fast lane, Mickey knew this was a part to which he could relate.

He does a good job in the film portraying the switch to an entirely different life as Francis finds God then dedicates his life to helping the poor. That was partly thanks to director Liliana Cavani having the right combination of patience and faith to get the best out of Mickey. One scene called for him, as Francis, to stand on a mountain-top willing God to speak to him and then suffering an emotional breakdown when it doesn't happen. Method actor Mickey just couldn't get into the right mood emotionally, even after nearly two hours of working up to it and, with time being money on a film set, some members of the crew started to look at their watches wondering when he would ever be ready to film a take. But Liliana came over and told him, 'Forget about the time, fuck the time, you take all the time you want.' Mickey was grateful and went back to his preparation. As he had the line, 'Oh Father . . .' he started to think about his own father and that familiar picture of his dad in the bodybuilding pose. He looked to the skies thinking about how much he wished his own father would appear from the heavens and speak to him. That made Mickey ready to shoot the scene and he nailed a perfect take.

He had so much belief in Cavani that he later agreed to her request to shoot an extra scene for the film where he rolls around naked in the snow to cleanse himself symbolically of his sins – something he might not have done for other directors. He was less pleased about his decision when he found a paparazzi photographer had sneaked on to the set and later sold pictures of the naked cleansing to a magazine.

While his performance in *Francesco* is suitably serene, the low-budget film is somewhat let down by Mickey having a late 1980s haircut. It also seems odd that while the rest of the cast deliver their lines in English accents, Mickey uses his own speaking voice.

Director Liliana Cavani's decision to dramatise a series of incidents from the saint's life rather than structure the film with a coherent narrative doesn't make for easy viewing and the movie was little seen and quickly for-gotten. Not that a movie about a saint finding God was ever going to be as big a hit as something with sex, violence and explosions.

After making back-to-back independent films for com-paratively little pay, Mickey welcomed a return to big-budget studio pictures – not least because the seven-figure salary would help out with his expensive tastes. But he was careful to pick out a fascinating character to play and chose well with *Johnny Handsome* (1989) an under-rated revenge thriller which saw him cast as a most unusual criminal and wearing heavy prosthetic make-up for the opening scenes.

In a role originally intended for Al Pacino, who dropped out due to not being satisfied with the script, Mickey played career criminal John Sedley who has a severely disfigured face until kind-hearted prison surgeon Dr Steven Fisher (Forest Whitaker) operates on him and gives the convict a handsome new face. When he leaves prison with a chance for a new life, Johnny just wants to get back at the double-crossing crooks who left him to be arrested and locked up, so he uses his new identity to lure them to their doom. Director Walter Hill cranks up the excitement, Morgan Freeman is brilliant as a cynical cop and Mickey brings power and pathos to his character's journey.

But although his performance was terrific, acting had lost its excitement for Mickey. It was becoming a boring, unfulfilling job for him. And when *Johnny Handsome* bombed at the box office, it was another disappointing setback.

His next movie, *Wild Orchid* (1990) was pretty awful but proved a happy experience for Mickey as he fell head-over-heels in love with his co-star, mouthwatering model Carré Otis. She played young lawyer Emily Reed who travels to sultry Rio de Janeiro on business and meets Mickey's character, mysterious and seductive millionaire business-man James Wheeler, who exposes her to a world of steamy perversions and various sexual shenanigans. It was a kind of low-rent 9½ *Weeks* and was directed, and co-written, by that film's co-writer, soft-core king Zalman King.

In the film, Mickey gets to looks moody, wear nice

clothes, ride his Harley Davidson and deliver some dreadful dialogue during a performance which would see him nominated as Worst Actor at that year's Golden Raspberry Awards for the biggest disasters in cinema. There was a far from convincing performance from Otis whose well-educated character supposedly speaks six languages, but Carré even struggles with her native English. She looks good, though, which is perhaps more important in this kind of film.

The movie is most remembered for its passion-packed, climactic nude sex scene where Mickey and Carré were rumoured to have had sex for real. The 'did they or didn't they?' intrigue was good PR and perhaps helped *Wild Orchid* to avoid utter embarrassment at the box office and escape with moderate takings.

Much better entertainment was provided by Mickey's next cinematic outing, crime thriller *Desperate Hours* (1990). The movie was a remake of a 1955 film of the same title and saw Mickey in the lead role originally played by Humphrey Bogart. His character, Michael Bosworth, is an escaped con on the run from the law who hides out in a married couple's suburban home and proceeds to terrorise the family. Anthony Hopkins is excellent as usual as the head of the family and his scenes with Mickey really crackle. The film gave Mickey the opportunity to work again with one of his favourite directors, Michael Cimino, but – as with their previous efforts together – this one flopped, too.

Next came the leading candidate for worst movie of Mickey's career, the embarrassment that was *Harley Davidson and the Marlboro Man* (1991). Ironically, it saw him earn the biggest salary of his career – $2.6 million – thanks to some ace negotiating by his then agent, Rick Nicita of CAA. Mickey knew that the material was bad but the fee was very attractive – especially as he had to pay for his big house, big cars and big entourage.

There's no shame in taking roles in rubbish films just for the large salary. Bigger stars than Mickey Rourke have been there and done that. Whenever Michael Caine would get a bad review, he would tell the press, 'OK, the movie was terrible, but the house I bought for my mother is beautiful.'

But Mickey hated himself for taking the movie purely for the money and quickly fell out of love with the movie business altogether. It's no wonder, given the weak plotting and mindless violence of a film which sees his character, Harley Davidson (like the bike he rides), team up with smoking cowboy pal, Marlboro Man (a lousy Don Johnson), and turn to crime so they can raise money to save their favourite bar from closure. In between shootouts and fight scenes, the stars are saddled with dialogue so bad that this makes *Scooby Doo* look like Shakespeare.

Audiences quite rightly ignored the movie, directed by Simon Wincer, and while Mickey had made a lot of money from the picture he had lost all respect for himself. He decided the only way he could win it back was in the boxing ring and made the startling decision at this time to become a professional fighter. The former amateur boxer had long wanted to get back into the fight game and knew he would be too old if he waited any longer.

But before he could put on the gloves, Mickey had one last contractual obligation to Hollywood, crime thriller *White Sands* (1992). Starting with the discovery in the desert of a suitcase full of cash next to a man's dead body, the story twists and turns its way into a fairly standard thriller which gets a burst of energy whenever Mickey is on screen giving his intense performance as the shady and sinister Gorman Lennox. He was surrounded by good talent in this one, such as director Roger Donaldson and co-star Samuel L. Jackson, but Mickey just wasn't motivated by acting in movies any more.

His future, at least in the short term, was going to be all about boxing . . . and Mickey couldn't wait to get in the ring.

3

Lord of the Ring

Mickey Rourke nervously paced the dressing room at the War Memorial Auditorium in Fort Lauderdale, Florida, as he prepared to make his professional boxing début.

It was 23 May 1991 and he was about to face journeyman fighter and part-time car mechanic Steve Powell in a four-round contest. There would be no second take if he screwed up here. Playing make-believe in movies was over – this was all too real.

Adding to Mickey's anxiety was the fact that he had suffered a hand injury before the bout. He didn't want to cancel and upset both the promoters and the public, so he decided to suck it up, fight on and go for it.

A packed house of 2,300 fans, curious to see if the Hollywood actor – who had arrived at the venue in a white limousine – could really cut it in the boxing ring, were first treated to other fights involving the likes of fighting physician Dr Harold 'Hackie' Reitman and world cruiser-weight champ Phil 'Enforcer' Jackson.

But, finally, it was the main event of the evening and

Mickey, weighing in at 178lb, emerged ready to do battle, wearing a a pair of gold satin shorts emblazoned with green shamrocks.

He was applauded to the ring by an audience relieved that he hadn't done what many suspected he might – lose his nerve and chicken out of the contest.

What followed was a scrappy, stop-start fight with Mickey starting out tentatively but gradually getting into his stride and making up for in enthusiasm what he lacked in finesse. Restricted by his injury, he fought dirty with a few nasty tricks picked up in various boxing gyms down the years.

'Sometimes you do what you have to do,' he told me recently when we discussed that first fight. It worked for him and he won the fight on the judges' decision.

The crowd, many of whom were Vietnam veterans, weren't wildly impressed with his showboating, dancing around the ring, street brawl-type punches and dirty tactics, some of them booing and others chanting 'Mi-ckey sucks', but Mickey loved every minute.

Originally, Mickey had only planned to have one professional boxing match, but following the début victory, the sport was back in his blood and it became the main focus of his life.

His ambition rapidly grew to win a title. He didn't get that but he did get self-respect – along with a succession of severe facial injuries.

■　　■　　■

It was on the set of his boxing movie, *Homeboy*, that Mickey first got the idea to return to the ring as a professional fighter. The climactic fight sequence just wasn't working out as choreographed – everything just looked clumsy and fake. So the star decided to throw away the script and improvise his own moves by boxing his equally enthusiastic opponent, a real fighter, for real to add authenticity to the film's ending. Suddenly, all the excitement of those amateur fights came rushing back to him and, as he threw and took actual punches, he felt gloriously alive.

Looking back, Mickey feels he should have made the switch to pro boxing there and then. Instead, he stayed in acting for a further three years. But film work wasn't making him happy. He longed for the unscripted adrenaline rush of boxing that would make him feel good about himself again. After all, when the bell rings, you can't say, 'I'm not emotionally ready,' or ask for more make-up to be applied – it's raw, rough and real, man against man, with no Hollywood bullshit.

When 1991 rolled around, Mickey realised he wasn't getting any younger and it would have to be now or never. To see if he still had fight skills, he went back to Miami's Fifth Street Gym for the first time in many years and sparred with various boxers there. He loved it, felt totally at home and found he hadn't lost his ring ability. That's when he took the decision which stunned Hollywood – to swap films for fights. He then persuaded respected boxing insider Tommy Torino to manage him and fix him up with a professional fight.

The switch to boxing was more about self-respect than stardom and Mickey chose not to fight under his famous name. Instead, he hoped to enter the ring as Romeo Florentino, which sounded like a good fighter's name to him. But the promoters of his contests wouldn't hear of it.

They were paying good money for Mickey Rourke, and therefore they wanted his recognisable – and bankable – name on the posters.

So he settled on adding a middle name: 'Marielito'. It was a Cuban nickname and he chose it as mark of respect to the tough Cuban kids he had grown up with, and fought with, in Miami. Marielito was a term applied to the 125,000 Cuban boat people who fled to the US in 1980 as part of an exodus of refugees from the Cuban port of Mariel. Al Pacino's title character in the 1983 movie *Scarface* was a fictional Marielito.

Mickey 'Marielito' Rourke fought eight professional bouts around the world in arenas ranging from Argentina to the Bahamas, Germany to Japan. Many of the audiences came out of curiosity and even a desire to see the Hollywood star beaten up, but Mickey held his own, won their respect and emerged with an unbeaten record. That was despite the fact that he was a pretty lazy trainer much of the time. Not for him was the fighter's discipline of getting up at six every morning and going for a long run. He was more inclined to do a bit of gym work, then have a rest, hit the punchbag and then have a cigarette.

But things gradually improved under the guidance of the leading fight trainer he hired to knock him into shape and make him a winner. Freddie Roach, a former boxer himself, knew what he was talking about and is today widely considered the best in the business as trainer to the likes of Manny Pacquiao and Amir Khan. Roach took a no-nonsense approach with Mickey and even quit in despair at one point when the actor-turned-boxer stayed out all-night partying when he was supposed to be resting and training. 'I don't train fighters to lose,' were his parting words.

But Mickey begged him to stay and promised to do better. He even wept in front of the trainer, which showed Freddie how much the fight game meant to him. Mickey knuckled down to his training back at the Fifth Street Gym in Miami, where his amateur fight career had started, and eventually found greater reserves of stamina and skill which got him through his super-middleweight fights.

In the gym, he sparred with, and got beaten around by, up-and-coming fighter James 'Lights Out' Toney who would later go on to beat the great Evander Holyfield. Toney managed to break his cheekbone, even though Mickey had a headguard on when they sparred. But those sessions toughened up Mickey and improved his ring craft.

His results and performances became impressive – he scored a first-round knockout over Darrell Miller in Japan, KO'd Thomas McCoy in three rounds in Germany and did the same in Spain to Terry 'The Hook' Jesmer.

Other celebrities have switched to short-lived sports careers with varying levels of success – from glamour model Jordan taking up dressage and polo to actress Geena Davis narrowly missing out on a place is the US archery team for the Sydney Olympics. But none have had the run of consistently good results that Mickey had – except for late acting legend Paul Newman who won several times as a race car driver, finished second in the Le Mans 24 Hour Race and entered the *Guinness Book of Records* as the oldest driver ever to win a professional motor race when he won the Daytona 24 Hours at the age of 70.

Mickey loved his time boxing professionally, particularly

for the mixture of electricity and fear he felt each time he was about to enter the ring. It was therapeutic for him after all the recent pain and frustration in his life. After all those years of scripted movies and several takes, he now had the strange thrill of not knowing what was going to happen next. When the bell sounded, it was like the moment a film camera's red light went on and he knew he had to deliver.

He also brought showbiz panache to the sport – entering to Guns 'n' Roses hit 'Sweet Child o' Mine' and sometimes fighting in multi-coloured shorts designed by Gianni Versace. Hollywood pals would show up at his fights and his *Pope of Greenwich Village* co-star Eric Roberts was among his most enthusiastic supporters.

Mickey shook up a sport that was running short of charismatic figures at that time and even made it on to the cover of prestigious magazine *World Boxing* in June 1994.

Mickey the boxer became a box-office draw and, despite getting only $250 for his first pro fight, eventually earned more than $1 million from his boxing career. He wanted to supplement his income – and expensive lifestyle – with the occasional film role but that proved tricky because he couldn't get an insurance bond. In other words, because he was fighting at the same time, the risk was too great and companies were extremely reluctant to insure a film with him in it.

But he was happy enough travelling the globe as a pro fighter. Hollywood came back to him when red-hot director Quentin Tarantino, a huge Mickey Rourke fan, offered Mickey a key role in *Pulp Fiction* as Butch Coolidge, a veteran boxer bribed by a mobster to throw his latest fight. It was a great role, perfect for Mickey, and could have catapulted him right back to the movie big time, but he didn't even read the script. He was preparing for a fight in Kansas against Tom Bentley at the time and didn't want to be distracted. After Mickey passed on the part, action star Bruce Willis got the role of Butch instead. He did a good job but surely the acclaimed movie would have been even more authentic and entertaining with Mickey in the role.

Mickey knows now that passing on *Pulp Fiction* was a mistake but he had no regrets at the time – especially after he KO'd Bentley in the first round. He was getting a bigger rush from fighting than he had ever experienced in films. The crowds gradually warmed to him as well. As fight fans saw he was serious about the sport, they gave him their respect.

It was a little harder to win over the sportswriters. Newspaper reports from his fight career carried headlines like 'ROURKE'S LATEST FIGHT NOTHING BUT A FARCE' and 'FANS BOO ROURKE AFTER DRAW'. Some of the press in Miami thought he was the biggest fake tough guy to come out of Florida since Vanilla Ice. But the fans nevertheless turned out in big numbers to watch Mickey fight. He had crowds of 10,000 and 15,000 at some of his contests.

Mickey got an especially warm welcome when fighting in Japan, where he was as famous for his TV commercials as his movies. Mickey had shot big-money Asian market-only ads for Suntory whisky and Daihatsu cars. Mickey admires Japanese culture and once bought a Samurai sword in Tokyo. To this day, some of his most frenzied fans are the Japanese.

Sadly, they didn't see much of him in the ring as his fight

in the Tokyo Dome was over in just two minutes with his opponent Darrell 'Big Chief' Miller decked by a bizarre punch that was more of a fly-swatting move than a champion's blow, but it was nevertheless effective. It was just as well he finished that fight early as Marielito was really sick with 'flu that night and knew he wouldn't be able to last more than two rounds.

On a trip to Argentina, he got to meet one of his boxing heroes, Carlos Monzon. The legendary fighter was serving a prison sentence for killing his common-law wife. Mickey visited him in his Argentinian jail and even sparred a little with him in there.

Mickey was gradually being accepted and even embraced by the fight community in America and befriended legendary fighters like Evander Holyfield and Sugar Ray Leonard. As time went on, the film star-turned-fighter felt more comfortable in the company of sportsmen than movie people.

At one point in his boxing career, he turned to the biggest legend of them all for help. Mickey was so nervous about an upcoming fight in which he feared he was outmatched that he couldn't sleep at night and instead just lay in bed shaking and sweating. He decided to turn for advice to his old inspiration, Muhammad Ali. Mickey called up the champ's friend and official photographer Howard Bingham and asked him for the favour of getting Ali to call him in a bid to settle his nerves.

The next night, Ali came on the phone. He didn't remember Mickey from the Fifth Street Gym days in Miami but he understood what he was going through and spent 15–20 minutes on the phone to Mickey, calming him down and boosting his confidence. As a result, Mickey was fine in the fight.

Ali's health deteriorated in the later stages of his career, not so much because of the fights but as a legacy of all the sparring he had done in training for them. Mickey had the same problem. During his pro career, Mickey was sparring up to 30 rounds a week, not always while wearing head-gear as the headguards made him claustrophobic.

One of those sparring sessions was with boxing great Thomas Hearns and Mickey came to realise how that champion had earned the nickname 'Hit Man.' He hit Mickey so hard that he suffered delayed concussion, feeling it 10 hours afterwards at midnight. Mickey suddenly felt so sick that he tried to phone for a doctor, but his head was so messed up he couldn't make his fingers touch the number keys.

As his own fighting career wound down, Mickey began to experience symptoms of brain damage, being unable to remember what he had done the night before. In addition to short-term memory loss, he was experiencing problems with his balance. Frightened of suffering permanent brain damage – and disintegrating like the boxer he played in *Homeboy* – Mickey arranged to take a neurological exam. He failed it and the doctor insisted, 'You should stop fighting immediately.'

Punch-drunk Mickey begged him to let him carry on, saying he had three more fights scheduled and the third one would have been for a WBO championship belt – a prize which would have meant more to him than an Oscar. He told the neurologist, 'I just need to fight three more times.'

But the expert replied, 'Listen, you can't even get hit in the head one more time, your neuro is so bad.'

When he told the doctor how much he would be earning for his next fight, the surgeon replied, 'You won't be able to count it.'

Faced with the choice of quitting the ring or risking becoming a drooling vegetable, Marielito took the wise decision and threw in the towel.

His last fight, in 1994, was a draw with 'Irish' Sean Gibbons in Davie, Florida. After six wins and two draws, Mickey retired from the ring unbeaten but had sustained several injuries over the previous three years, including broken bones in each hand, broken ribs and a few concussions. Mickey had also sustained facial injuries which required several operations. These ranged from a split tongue to a compressed cheekbone. He ended up with far fewer teeth in his mouth than had been there beforehand and his nose was broken twice. Mickey needed five operations on his nose – which was rebuilt with cartilage taken from his ear.

Mickey's face was reconstructed by a cosmetic surgeon used by other boxers and nicknamed 'The Butcher'. During one of the procedures, The Butcher stuck a long needle into Mickey's lip and pulled out an infection. His work left Mickey's lip sticking out a long way. He was supposed to go back for one more corrective session with The Butcher after that but couldn't face the pain and never returned. It would take four years for his face to return to relative normality.

So Mickey emerged from the boxing years with a freakish appearance far different from his pretty-boy looks of the past. He had suffered the biggest facial collapse since those melting Nazis at the end of *Raiders of the Lost Ark*.

He looks better now but the legacy of those boxing batterings will be with him forever.

The nerve damage in his hands means he is unable to do anything intricate with them and the boxing had also had an affect on his walking, which was noticed when he kept tripping on his way to the stage at late 2008/early 2009 awards shows. He sometimes likes to go surfing but is lousy at it because his balance is so bad.

Boxing had given Mickey a discipline and a routine that his acting career has lacked and he knew he could take those tools with him into his future film work. But the sport had also messed up his looks and meant that resuming his movie career at the top level would not be as easy as he thought.

In fact, trying to make his way back to stardom would prove Mickey's toughest fight of all.

Mickey Rourke's Professional Boxing Record

6 Wins (4 knockouts, 2 decisions),

0 Losses, 2 Draws

Res.	Record	Opponent	Type	Rd., Time	Date	Location	Notes
Win	1-0	Steve Powell	Unanimous decision	4	May 23, 1991	Fort Lauderdale, Florida, USA	Scoring was 38-37, 38-37 and 39-37
Win	2-0-1	Darrell Miller	TKO	1 (4) 2:14	June 23, 1991	Tokyo, Japan	
Draw	1-0-1	Francisco Harris	Majority draw	4	April 25, 1992	Miami Beach, Florida, USA	Scoring was 38-39 for Harris, 38-38 and 38-38
Win	3-0-1	Terry Jesmer	Decision	4	December 12, 1992	Oviedo, Spain	
Win	4-0-1	Tom Bentley	TKO	1 (4)	March 30, 1993	Kansas City, Missouri, USA	
Win	5-0-1	Bubba Stotts	TKO	3 (4)	July 24, 1993	Joplin, Missouri, USA	
Win	6-0-1	Thomas McCoy	TKO	3 (4)	November 20, 1993	Hamburg, Germany	
Draw	6-0-2	Sean Gibbons	Majority draw	4	September 8, 1994	Davie, Florida, USA	Scoring was 37-39 for Gibbons, 38-38 and 38-38

4

A Life on Screen – Part II

'What you need for this role is a Mickey Rourke type,' the Hollywood studio executive told Francis Ford Coppola.

The legendary director had been discussing the casting of a key character in his new movie, *The Rainmaker*, with bosses from Paramount, the studio for whom he had made *The Godfather* 25 years earlier. A little confused by the 'Rourke type' comment, Coppola said, 'But Mickey is still out there, still working ... why not just get him?'

The room fell silent. The Paramount people looked at each other uncomfortably. Mickey was trouble, wasn't he? A hell-raising headcase. Was he really still working? Certainly his recent roles, raging from a gay bank robber to a flamboyant psychiatrist, were in films barely seen by anyone.

What Mickey needed was someone with authority and talent to give him another shot at the big time – and Coppola, who had directed him in *Rumble Fish* and had long championed the actor, was prepared to be that person. Ignoring the sceptics in the room, he insisted Mickey was the right man for the role – and Mickey responded with a great performance in *The Rainmaker*. That was the first step in a long and winding road back to the top.

■   ■   ■

Mickey didn't entirely abandon acting during his boxing years. He made three films in that period – all of which were set around bank robberies. The first was a TV movie for US cable channel HBO called *The Last Outlaw* (1993). It was a Western, set in 1880, shot in Santa Fe, New Mexico, and saw Mickey riding a horse while wearing a 10-gallon hat, chaps and spurs and toting guns.

He plays the lead role of Graff, head of a ruthless gang of former Confederate soldiers who rob banks and kill anyone who gets in their way. When the gang betrays him, Graff sets out to hunt down each of his treacherous enemies and violently kills them one by one. It was directed by Geoff Murphy who had previous experience of Westerns having been behind the camera on *Young Guns 2*. But this one was let down by its slow pace and never came close to the superior quality of other productions on HBO, the channel behind *The Sopranos*, *Band of Brothers*, *Sex and the City* and a string of award winning TV movies. It was fun, though, to see Mickey playing a 19th-century renegade.

Next came *F.T.W.* (1994) also known as *The Last Ride*, a downbeat movie, co-written by Mickey under his now grander pen name of 'Sir' Eddie Cook – who, in an inside joke, had apparently been knighted since writing *Homeboy*. In the film he plays rodeo rider Frank T. Wells (the initials of the title, which was also supposed to stand for 'Fuck The World') who has just been released from prison after serving a term for manslaughter and is trying to get back into the old routine when he meets and falls for Scarlett Stuart (played by Lori Singer), an emotionally disturbed, beautiful bank robber on the run who changes his life – but not necessarily for the better. Although Mickey was thrilled to see his second script produced, it was a blow when *F.T.W.* failed to make it on to cinema screens and went straight to video.

Fall Time (1995) found him playing a gay bank robber named Florence. Seriously! This surreal crime film set in 1950s America starts with Florence declaring his love for his partner in crime and life, played by Stephen Baldwin, and, by the end of the movie, both characters will be dead. The gay storyline isn't really developed in the form of any love scenes – this is no *Brokeback Bank Job* – as the homosexuality takes second place to the heist. In the end, it's just a strange little shoot-'em-up featuring some more outlaw posturing from Mickey and not the kind of film which would return him to the big time.

When he hung up his boxing gloves, Mickey knew he had the talent to be an acting champion again but just wanted the opportunity to show his skills alongside the big names of the time. He said back then, 'You put me in something with Alec Baldwin or Daniel Day-Lewis or Kevin Costner and I'll eat their assholes.'

Instead of that award-winning trio of actors, his next few co-stars included Jean Claude van Damme, Tupac Shakur and, once again, Carré Otis. *Exit in Red* (1996) marked the uneagerly awaited reteaming of Mickey and Otis for the first time on screen since *Wild Orchid*. He plays a psychiatrist and she co-stars as the lawyer who loves him but there are few sexual sparks between them this time, not least because Mickey's character is more attracted to a femme fatale, played by B-movie actress Annabel Schofield, who ends up framing him for murder. Because he has a chequered past himself, the shrink struggles to convince the authorities he is innocent and has to take matters into his own hands. The movie is silly throughout and Mickey fails to convince as an experienced psychiatrist, sporting long blond hair, foppish clothes, sunglasses and smoking through a long cigarette holder.

He had a much harder look in his next film, a gritty and violent crime drama shot and set on the mean streets of Brooklyn , called *Bullet* (1996). It was co-written by Mickey, again under the name of Sir Eddie Cook, with Bruce Rubenstein, whose family background inspired the story. Mickey also served as music supervisor on *Bullet*, overseeing a varied soundtrack that veered from Vivaldi to Right Said Fred and Barry White to hip-hop. His boxing trainer, Freddie Roach, was hired as fight co-ordinator for the film.

Mickey took the lead role of self-destructive heroin addict Butch 'Bullet' Stein who gets out of prison and straight back into trouble, robbing junkies and stabbing a drug-dealer in the eye. His friend John Enos III plays his best mate in the movie, and future Oscar winner Adrien Brody is the sensitive and artistic little brother whom Bullet is desperate to protect at all costs.

But the most noteworthy co-star was rapper Tupac Shakur, playing feared local drug lord Tank, who fights a street war with Bullet and shoots him dead at the end after uttering the cool line, 'The music's over, motherfucker.'

Shakur and Mickey bonded well during filming and

found lots in common, both of them being perceived as bad boys but possessing the souls of poets. However, their friendship was not to last long as, in September 1996, after seeing a Mike Tyson fight in Las Vegas, Tupac was the victim of a drive-by shooting. He was struck in the chest, pelvis, right hand and thigh and died from his injuries several days later. The tragedy hit Mickey hard and Mickey still keeps a picture of his slain friend in his home.

Although *Bullet*, released a month after Shakur's death, didn't do much at the box office, it had an authentic feel about it and Mickey could be proud of the movie. It is hard to say the same about his next effort, though, which was the action flick *Double Team* (1997).

A mix of martial arts mayhem, massive explosions, poor plotting and dismal dialogue, the movie was a bit of a joke but, to his credit, Mickey took it seriously and underwent rigorous martial arts training and strenuous bodybuilding to prepare for the fight scenes, many of them shirtless, required in his role as international terrorist Stavros. His co-stars were the 'Muscles from Brussels' action star Jean Claude Van Damme, as an anti-terrorist agent, and tattooed basketball bad-boy-turned-reality TV star Dennis Rodman, playing a flamboyant arms dealer who inserts basketball jargon into most of his lame lines. Van Damme's character spends much of the movie trying to eliminate Mickey's and there's a fun showdown between them at the end in an ancient coliseum rigged with land mines. The flop film's cheesiest but most gloriously entertaining moment comes when Mickey Rourke sends a man-eating tiger against Jean Claude Van Damme only for the pocket dynamo from Brussels to defend himself by kicking the charging beast.

It must have seemed like a good idea at the time to make *Another 9½ Weeks* (1997). Mickey needed a hit and a sequel to his biggest ever box-office success would seem to fit the bill. But Kim Basinger wasn't going to return – she had bigger fish to fry having just filmed her Oscar-winning role in *LA Confidential*. So the absence of her character, Elizabeth, would have to be dealt with in the script. Set ten years after the original, the sequel sees Mickey's character, John Gray, pining for his lost love and following her trail to Paris only to find Elizabeth has died. But he gets over his disappointment by having a fling with her best friend, played by model Angie Everhart, who has read Elizabeth's diary and is well up for some of the same sex play with John. He is soon covering her naked body in rose petals, red wine and honey, but Mickey's heart isn't in it this time. The quality isn't there either, and this follow-up film doesn't come remotely close to the excitement, atmosphere or eroticism of the original.

Just when it seemed Mickey's post-boxing acting comeback was going nowhere, Francis Ford Coppola suddenly called and offered him a potentially career-reviving role in his major new movie *The Rainmaker* (1997). Mickey knew studio chiefs had been hesitant but Coppola had fought to add him to a cast including much hotter names like Matt Damon, Clare Danes and Danny DeVito. He wasn't going to let him down.

Grateful for the opportunity and delighted to be working again with the director who Mickey judges all others against, Mickey gave a scene-stealing performance in the prestige project, and it was John Grisham himself who would call this the best screen adaptation of one of his books.

Sporting greased back silver hair, a neat goatee beard, yellow-tinted sunglasses and sharp suits, Mickey is fun to watch as Bruiser Stone, a slick, shifty and shrewd veteran lawyer who gives Matt Damon's law student character a job with his minor law firm which leads to the rookie landing the case of a lifetime. Mickey was so entertaining that audiences who viewed the film at preview test screenings kept saying they wanted to see more of his character. So Coppola gave them their wish by calling Mickey back to shoot extra scenes which were edited into the final cut. Up to this point, Mickey had generally chosen not to attend premières of his movies as, in common with other perfectionist actors, he doesn't like watching himself on screen – but he made an exception for this one and liked what he saw.

The Rainmaker made $50 million at the US box office but being in a hit didn't give Mickey the kind of career boost he might have expected. Instead of offers from other major studios and leading directors, he was catapulted back to the world of low-budget and often lower-quality movies, starting with a small role in *Buffalo '66* (1998).

This bleak drama with a meagre budget of $1.5 million was written by, directed and starred Vincent Gallo as a young man just out of prison who managed to hide the fact he was in jail from his dysfunctional parents who think instead that he got married and went to work far away. When he goes to visit them, he needs a woman to pretend to be his bride and kidnaps a tap dancer, played by Christina Ricci, whom he forces to play the part.

Mickey, in the role of a sleazy and vengeful bookie, is only in the movie for a few minutes but still manages to act everyone else off the screen. His character was owed $10,000 by Gallo over a losing bet on the Buffalo Bills in the SuperBowl and, when he couldn't pay, had forced him to take the fall for one of his criminal cronies and serve the prison sentence.

The story of how he came to participate in the film is just as entertaining as anything in the movie. Mickey was struggling for cash at the time – owing money on back taxes among other things – and was finding it hard to get hired for movies. Vincent Gallo understood the situation and had a neat solution – offering to pay Mickey $100,000 in cash to be in *Buffalo '66*. Mickey got straight on a plane to Buffalo, New York, did his work for four hours, and left with a paper bag full of money.

American movie stars generally don't like to take on TV work, believing it is a step down and lowers their mystique, but then again beggars can't be choosers and hard-up Mickey took on the lead part in a US cable TV film called *Thicker Than Blood* (1998) both for the money and the welcome opportunity to play a nice-guy role. He gives a good, sensitive performance as Father Frank Larkin, a Catholic priest trying to help troubled street kids in his parish. Given his Catholic background, Mickey looked comfortable in the role and elevated the material with some underplayed acting.

Next came another brief but flashy performance in crime thriller *Thursday* (1998), a kind of *Pulp Fiction* wannabe in which Mickey shows up as a bad guy named Khasarov. He is one of a series of hoods who come calling after a former drug-dealer-gone-straight, played by Thomas Jane, makes the mistake of allowing his heroin-dealer mate, played by Aaron Eckhart, to stay at his place for a few days. Despite the good cast and some interesting ideas, the film made no impact.

Then it was violence all the way in *Point Blank* (1998) which sees a busload of dangerous criminals take over a Texan shopping mall and shoot every shopper, security guard or cop who comes anywhere near them. Into this mayhem wades Mickey's pumped-up character, Ruby Ray, who plans to rescue his escaped convict brother from the centre of the carnage by going all *Die Hard* and fighting a one-man war against all-comers. Former real-life jailbird and boxer Danny Trejo, who would later star with Mickey in both *Animal Factory* and *Once Upon a Time in Mexico*, is also fun to watch as the toughest of the bad guys but otherwise the movie is just lots and lots of mindless butchery.

Suddenly, a passage from under-par B-movies to artistic epics opened up as Mickey got the kind of out-of-the-blue offer that great actors dream about. Reclusive but brilliant director Terrence Malick wanted him for a role in his long awaited World War II film *The Thin Red Line* (1998), which was to be the meticulous moviemaker's first picture in 20 years.

Every actor in Hollywood was keen on being part of this landmark project about the conflict in the South Pacific and it was a great tribute to Mickey that he got selected as part of the large ensemble cast while bigger stars who had chased after roles, including Tom Cruise, Leonardo Di Caprio and Robert De Niro, did not.

So Mickey headed off to Australia for the filming with high hopes for his role as a battle scarred soldier and was thrilled to be working with Malick, a cinematic craftsman who had won his respect with 1975 classic *Badlands*.

But it was all to end in disappointment as Mickey's role was eventually spliced out of the final cut. He wasn't alone – the same thing happened to Gary Oldman, Viggo Mortensen and Billy Bob Thornton as the director edited down his five-hour cut to the contracted running time of under three hours.

Mickey does get thanked in the end credits but that was little consolation. He felt he gave one of his best ever performances in *The Thin Red Line* and yet no one got to see it. Meanwhile, the rambling film fared badly at the box office while becoming a favourite with critics, and landed seven Oscar nominations but no wins.

Short of money and good opportunities, he drifted from one low-budget film to another, making the kind of movies destined for the DVD discount bins rather than the big screen.

These included the forgettable drama *Cousin Joey* (1999) – produced by action star Steven Seagal and directed by fashion designer Sante D'Orazio – which is about a pair of drug addicts caught up in the New York underworld.

Shergar (1999) was inspired by the mystery disappearance of the great racehorse of the same name and imagined what might have happened to the Derby winner. Sightings of the movie have been as rare as glimpses of the stallion himself in recent years but it's worth tracking down as the film is actually quite involving and intriguing. Mickey plays Gavin O'Rourke, a member of an IRA terror cell who kidnap the horse and hold him for ransom, only for a young stable boy to foil their plans.

His next effort, *Out in Fifty* (1999), also had its moments. Another low-budget crime drama, this one found Mickey as vengeful Jack Bracken, a pill-popping, hard-drinking cop hunting down the man who killed his wife. But, again, few people saw it.

Even fewer saw *Shades* (1999), an odd film that's now hard to find and not really worth the effort. A Belgian picture shot in Antwerp and Brussels, it stars Mickey as down-on-his-luck Hollywood film director Paul S. Sullivan who goes to Belgium and makes a movie over there for the money – a case of art imitating life perhaps? The movie within a movie shows the film business to be full of unscrupulous producers and prima donna stars – so they certainly got that part right.

Could it get any more bizarre for Mickey than a low-budget movie in Belgium? Absolutely. When Steve Buscemi called him up and offered Mickey the part of a transvestite in a prison movie he was directing, Mickey thought his old co-star from *The Last Outlaw* was joking. Surely he wanted him to play a standard tough guy convict. He only realised Steve was serious when the script for *Animal Factory* (2000) turned up in his mail box with a note asking him to look at the part of flamboyant jailbird Jan the Actress. Buscemi really rated Mickey as an actor and knew that that role would require someone terrific to make it seem real rather than a joke. Mickey found himself intrigued by the idea of playing a character described as a muscular transvestite with green fingernails, thick lipstick and a lisp. He saw it as a true acting challenge – and Mickey really committed to the role.

For the performance, he used his memories of his early days in LA working as a bouncer in the transvestite club. He had also worked in one in Miami when he was 18, so he knew the cursing, lisping, muscular tranny types and went all out to turn himself into one of them for the film. He had his dentist take out the fixed bridge that keeps his two fake front teeth in place and that helped him achieve the lisp. Next he went to a Beverly Hills nail salon for a French manicure and then had his eyebrows waxed and reshaped so they were higher and longer. He also had his hair cut extremely short.

Continuing his usual tradition of picking out his own outfits for roles, he went to famous adults-only LA shops like Trashy Lingerie and The Pleasure Chest and bought a red satin bra and red g-string to wear in the film. As he visited other lingerie stores and boutiques over the course of ten days, trying on women's clothes, Mickey would get strange looks – especially from customers and staff who recognised him. He even ended up in the tabloids as speculation grew about his strange shopping habits.

But Mickey shrugged it all off and got on with continuing to assemble his cross-dressing convict look – which he did by cutting the sleeves off an old blue cowboy-style shirt and tying it up at the waist, adding some hip-hugging jeans and powder-blue shoes with spiked heels and fur on the front. He completed the ensemble by having a belly ring put in – a piercing which hurt like hell. Then, to get into character, he went and flew on the plane from LA to Vancouver wearing his full outfit and make-up for the film.

The movie, adapted from his book by one of Steve Buscemi's *Reservoir Dogs* co-stars, ex-con Edward Bunker, sees Edward Furlong playing a first-time offender thrown into a prison with a bunch of freaks and tough guys including characters played by previous Mickey Rourke co-stars Willem Dafoe and Danny Trejo. Mickey's best moment in the film is a memorable monologue – which he wrote himself – where Jan talks about wanting to become a butterfly and flying beyond the prison bars then all the way to Paris. The lines were inspired by Mickey reasoning that institutionalised characters like Jan would try to cope with their situation by living in their heads and indulging in just such delusional fantasies.

Mickey was rewarded for his efforts with some terrific reviews but there were to be no large audiences for the grim picture about prison life. With his career in trouble, Mickey was really low on cash and on the lookout for a role in a big-budget movie which could get him back on track. Then a guardian angel walked across his path, in the rather unlikely form of Sylvester Stallone.

The Rocky and Rambo superstar was dining in an Italian restaurant, saw Mickey eating alone at a nearby table, free of the usual entourage which had surrounded him in the past, and went over to offer him a job in his next movie, *Get Carter* (2000). Stallone told him, 'Listen, I'm doing this movie and I need somebody in it who looks like they can kick my ass. You look like you can kick my ass.'

Mickey, who could barely afford to pay for the bowl of spaghetti he was eating, eagerly accepted the job as villain-ous club owner Cyrus Paice in Sly's remake of the classic 1971 Michael Caine crime film. But when the contract came through, the money on offer was so startlingly low that Mickey found it disrespectful and turned the job down . . . but thanked Stallone for the offer anyway. That Mickey did end up in the film was all down to Stallone's generosity. When the producer couldn't or wouldn't pay Mickey what he felt he was worth, Sly doubled Mickey's salary by chipping in the extra money out of his own pocket.

But while the money was right in the end, the film wasn't – from Stallone's strange goatee beard to the jerky camera movements and underwhelming script, there was something not quite right about it. Stallone plays mob enforcer Jack Carter who sets out to seek and kill those responsible for his brother's murder. But it's just not a patch on the rough, tough original and Michael Caine's appearance in a cameo reminds viewers of that fact. Still, the *Get Carter* remake was a million times better than Mickey's next movie.

It is to be hoped that Mickey Rourke's fortunes never again sink so low that he has to take a role in another crummy killer insect movie like *They Crawl* (2001). He appears in one scene as weirdo Tiny Frakes, trying to mislead a police detective that he knows nothing about a series of murders caused by a rampaging posse of genetically mutated cockroaches. The movie is so bad on every level that it leaves you wondering how films like this even get made.

Mickey's titanic career was sinking fast now – but then Sean Penn threw him a lifeline. Penn was directing the haunting, intense drama *The Pledge* (2001), starring Jack Nicholson as a veteran detective trying to solve the murder of a little girl, and hired some of the best actors around for cameo appearances, including Benicio Del Toro, Helen Mirren, Vanessa Redgrave . . . and Mickey Rourke. Mickey's role was that of James Olstad, the grieving and tormented father of another murdered child who now goes through the motions working as a janitor in a rest home. In his one scene, acting opposite Jack Nicholson, Mickey reminded Hollywood just what a powerful actor he was, getting every ounce of emotion out of his tale of loss.

Mickey was thrilled to be back acting alongside a real talent like Jack Nicholson, whom he thought was very generous and giving in the scene, by taking a back seat and allowing him to shine. He worked for three months preparing for that one day's work – and it's an acting masterclass. The film doesn't follow the conventions of most psychological thrillers but is a thought-provoking and well-made piece of work.

It was back to lower-quality stuff for Mickey's next movie, *Picture Claire* (2001), a 'wrong time, wrong place' thriller starring Juliette Lewis as a woman who gets mistaken for a killer and ends up fleeing both the police and some vengeful drug-dealers. Gina Gershon co-stars as the real murderer and Mickey is third in the credits, but doesn't hang around long, as her victim, Eddie, a toothpick-chewing, leather jacket-wearing, foul-mouthed criminal. His only scene is set in a doughnut shop where Juliette Lewis, as Claire, asks him for directions. Eddie doesn't want to be bothered, spills coffee over her, tells her to fuck off and calls her a cunt. While she is in the bathroom wiping coffee off her clothes, Eddie's lusty girlfriend Lily, played by Gina Gershon, comes into the now empty doughnut shop, straddles her lover and then strangles him with some wire before rushing out. The elderly store owner wrongly identifies Juliette's character as the killer and, confused, she goes on the run.

It's all fairly routine after that with the only other moment in the movie to watch out for being Tori Spelling's future husband Dean McDermott playing 'attendant at station' – very badly.

There was one amusing moment during filming in Toronto – although the moviemakers weren't laughing. They called for silence while shooting a street scene only for a woman to keep blowing a whistle, thereby ruining the takes. The phantom whistler was eventually arrested for causing a disturbance and taken away by the cops. But viewers can pretty much blow the whistle on this movie once Mickey's memorable scene is over.

Mickey had worked hard to banish his old hellraiser reputation and felt that his professionalism in recent movies like *The Pledge* and *Get Carter* could help him land the juicy roles he wanted in prestige projects. But he clearly hadn't done enough to impress some people, for Mickey lost out at this time on a lead role in the long-in-development erotic thriller *In the Cut* (2003) because Nicole Kidman, making her producing début on the film and given final approval on all casting decisions, didn't want him in the movie. Mickey was frustrated – especially as Kidman had discounted him without ever meeting him.

Mickey just needed someone to believe in him and help him towards the kind of opportunities his talent deserved. Enter his new agent – David Unger. Mickey didn't much like the script of the drugs movie *Spun* (2002) and, with the exception of Eric Roberts, had little interest in the cast but he made the movie anyway because his new agent told him to do so.

Mickey had put his career in the hands of the young man who wanted to chart a new course for his client, handpicking supporting roles for Mickey in films by up-and-coming directors that Unger said would lead him back to the big time. *Spun* was one of these projects, and was directed by Jonas Akerlund, who had shown a promising visual style as director of eye-catching pop videos like Madonna's 'Ray of Light' and U2's 'Beautiful Day'.

David Unger first met Mickey Rourke, and a few of his dogs, in a coffee shop, and treated him with great respect. Unger told him he was a young agent with a lot to prove and he believed in Mickey and asked Mickey to have the same belief in him. Some of his colleagues at ICM may have been sceptical, but Unger was confident he could bring about a comeback for his new client. Unger's grandfather was a movie producer, and the young agent was steeped in the movie business, having been brought up on films like *Rumble Fish, Diner* and *9½ Weeks*. He knew if he targeted directors of his same thirtysomething generation, they would feel the same way.

So he lined up meetings with those directors; Mickey would meet them, apologise for his past deeds and say he was ready to be reliable and become a movie star again. All these 'getting to know you' meetings were of the kind any promising young actor trying to make his way in Hollywood goes through – but Mickey was doing them as he approached middle-age.

The other things the new agent asked him to do to make him more appealing to moviemakers and casting agents was to stop lifting weights – so his neck wouldn't look so thick and his body be so pumped up. And he should stop wearing tank-tops and workout clothes everywhere and get his hair cut.

Unger and Mickey hit it off and became a good team and

trusting friends. When Unger's parents' dog died, Mickey got them another one – and they called it Mickey.

It would take a while but Unger's career strategy would eventually pay off and lead Mickey from obscurity to the awards circuit. To say thank you, Mickey gave David the Golden Globe award he won for *The Wrestler*.

But such glory seemed a long way away on *Spun*, in which Mickey played The Cook, a maker of the drug crystal meth who has set up a methamphetamine lab in a motel room and spends his days with spaced-out druggies. *Spun* was based on incidents from the life of the film's co-writer, Will De Los Santos, who once drove a meth cook around Eugene, Oregon, for three days.

The film is frantic – featuring a record 5,000 edits – bizarre and suitably trippy but Mickey swaggers through it at his own pace and steals the movie with a pair of memorable scenes. The first is comedic as The Cook delivers a monologue in an adult video store about the appreciation of 'pussy' and the second dramatic as he tells a story from childhood about his mother being unable to take care of him and wondering if she should have killed him.

The movie wasn't a financial success but it attracted plenty of publicity, Mickey did some promotion for it and the film got him back in the spotlight. Something else he got out of it was the striking pair of white cowboy boots he wears in the film. Mickey took such a shine to them that he had it written into his contract that he got to keep them at the end.

From Larry Charles, future director of *Borat* and *Brüno*, came the far less entertaining *Masked and Anonymous* (2003) starring Bob Dylan, in his first screen role in 16 years, as

Jake Fate, a legendary singer on a downward career spiral who makes a comeback at a benefit concert for victims of a war. Described as 'arty-farty' by Mickey Rourke, the film, co-written by Bob, lacks structure and sense but features a great supporting cast who were clearly keen to work with Dylan, even if they couldn't all comprehend the script. Those names include Penelope Cruz, Christian Slater, Val Kilmer, Ed Harris, John Goodman, Jessica Lange and Jeff Bridges, along with Mickey himself, well down the credits in the role of Edmund, a politician with a personal connection to Dylan's character.

There was a real-life connection, too. Dylan had been a longtime fan of Mickey's and describes in his memoirs, *Chronicles: Volume One*, of being blown away by his performance in *Homeboy*. Meanwhile, Mickey already knew Dylan a little – the iconic singer had been a customer back when he ran Mickey and Joey's, his Beverly Hills newsstand and café – but the pair of them bonded on the set of the movie. Dylan asked Mickey for acting advice after finding himself unsure what to do with his hands in scenes where he had no dialogue and Mickey told him to find some activity to do on screen. Ever since then, the legend has phoned Mickey every so often, usually late at night and always with the words, 'Hi, it's Bob . . .' causing a confused and sleepy Mickey to grunt, 'Bob who?' and getting the reply, 'You know . . . Bob!'

From Bob to Robert . . . It was director Robert Rodriguez who hired Mickey next and their relationship was to be a key factor in Mickey's return to the big time. It was working for him, first on *Once Upon a Time in Mexico* and then on *Sin City*, which really paved the way for Mickey's path back to success. The Texan moviemaker had been a fan of the actor for years. In his late teens, he used to practise editing techniques by splicing together scenes from *Rumble Fish*, *Angel Heart* and other Mickey Rourke movies that he loved. Even then, he dreamed of directing Mickey in a movie some day. But with little cash or connections, breaking into the film business would be tough.

But a lot can be achieved with determination and Robert went to great lengths to achieve his goal, culminating in the future director selling his body for science experiments to raise the cash for his directorial début *El Mariachi*. The success of that movie led to him directing other hits like *Desperado*, *From Dusk 'Til Dawn* and *Spy Kids* before he got the opportunity to make *Once Upon a Time in Mexico* (2003), a homage to the Sergio Leone Westerns he had grow up on.

The film, set around an attempted coup in Mexico, featured Antonio Banderas as a gunslinging guitarist and Johnny Depp as a corrupt CIA agent. But there was also a role for Mickey Rourke – who had been suggested to Rodriguez by Depp – as a shady character called Billy Chambers. It was only a small part but Rodriguez was so impressed with Mickey's work that he kept adding scenes so he could get more of Mickey on screen. He would write scenes for Mickey in his lunch break. An hour later, pages of great dialogue were waiting for the Rourke touch. Robert even let the star act with his dog Loki in the film.

When they had first met to discuss working together, Mickey had been holding Loki in his arms throughout their chat. Robert thought that could work in the movie, too, so decided to add the dog, renamed Moco for the film (which was the name of the villain in Robert's first picture, *El Mariachi*), to the script as Billy's only friend.

Something else Mickey brought with him to the shoot were his own clothes. Mickey has worn, or offered to wear, his own outfits in most of his movies down the years and *Once Upon a Time in Mexico*'s director – who was busy managing every aspect of the film – was delighted to get help with the costumes. He told Mickey to bring something 'cowboy' and was impressed when Mickey showed up with immaculate two-tone suits and cool cowboy hats. In fact, the blue designer suit Mickey wears in his character's final scene when he is shot dead was so nice that Robert didn't want to ruin it by putting a bullet hole in the jacket. So he spent more of the production's money creating a digital special effect of a bullet hole that was added in post-production in order to save Mickey's suit from being damaged.

Whereas Mickey's character gets killed – along with 98 other characters in the film – his dog doesn't, and that probably made the movie more popular. For there is a well-known rule in moviemaking circles that you can kill any amount of people on screen, but you will always lose the audience's affection for a film if you kill a dog.

Mickey had a good time filming scenes with old pals like Willem Dafoe and Danny Trejo but was especially impressed by director Robert Rodriguez's ability and enthusiasm – and the feeling was mutual. Robert would spread the word to his moviemaking pals that Mickey had a thoroughly professional attitude now.

As he got to know him better during filming, the director realised Mickey was a troubled soul and had a lot of pain to draw on in his performances. Robert filed that information away thinking it could come in useful for a project he was in the early stages of thinking about, called *Sin City*.

Mickey Rourke was gradually gaining a much better reputation for his behaviour on film sets and he wasn't about to ruin that after being cast in a prestige kidnap thriller starring Denzel Washington, *Man on Fire* (2004). He was professional in every way, such as sticking to the dialogue he was given rather than improvising different lines as he had done frequently on other films. Mickey was also among friends here working with the likes of co-star Christopher Walken and director Tony Scott. Mickey had long been one of Scott's favourite actors and the director, who likes to put actors in roles featuring elements of their own personalities, cast him as corrupt lawyer Jordan Kalfus feeling Mickey could bring his own strange mixture of sweet and dark to the part.

Scott had originally planned to make the movie 20 years earlier and set it in Italy which was the world kidnap capital at the time. That project fell through but when the chance came again to make the film, he switched the action to Mexico as there was an average of one kidnap every hour in 21st-century Latin America – and 70 per cent of those taken turn up dead. Against that background, *Man on Fire* sees Denzel's former CIA operative hired as a bodyguard to a nine-year-old girl, played by Dakota Fanning. But he can't stop her being snatched by Mexican kidnappers and the fight to bring her back leads to escalating action and intrigue.

Man on Fire took in $77 million at the US box office and remains to this day Mickey's biggest hit in the States . . .

and probably will stay so until *Iron Man 2* opens. Another smash hit was to follow – and it really put Mickey's career back on track.

After making the third film in his successful teen heroes trilogy, *Spy Kids*, Robert Rodriguez was looking for something more challenging and he found it in a film version of Frank Miller's popular and stylish graphic novels about cool criminals, crooked cops, dastardly villains and sexy dames, *Sin City* (2005).

For the key role of Marv, a hulking, hugely tall tough guy, he thought immediately of Mickey Rourke. The choice surprised Frank Miller, who was brought in as co-director. The comic book king said, 'Do you mean that skinny guy from *Body Heat*?' But Robert assured him the actor he had worked with on *Once Upon a Time in Mexico* was different now, looked physically imposing, could draw on his boxing years for the brute force needed in the fight scenes and, most importantly, was a great actor with a tortured mind who could really tap into the frustration of Marv, who spends the movie avenging the death of his one true love.

Mickey would have to have prosthetics over his face to recreate the look of the character in the graphic novel but, as a fan of *Johnny Handsome*, Rodriguez knew his choice had the ability to act through heavy make-up and bring emotion to the scenes. It was especially important that the acting did not get lost amid all the stunning visuals in the stylised film, which was all shot in front of a green screen with the backgrounds digitally added during post-production. With all the computers around the Austin, Texas, set, Mickey remarked that it was like acting in a NASA mission control room. But despite all the CGI trickery, Mickey's great performance gives the film a recognisably human element.

Mickey brought his own ideas to the role, including giving Marv a tough guy walk apparently borrowed from an IRA gunman he had met many years earlier in Ireland.

Because he doesn't like watching himself in movies, Mickey never normally looks at playbacks on monitors after filming scenes. But he made an exception on *Sin City* because, behind all that make-up, it was like watching someone else on camera.

He broke another habit here, too. Mickey had rarely done action scenes up to this point – choosing to let his stunt double do them instead rather than risk injuries – but he was happy to take them on in *Sin City*, particularly relishing a scene where Marv attacks a bunch of thugs with an axe.

Mickey's acting was on fire in this film, getting many of his scenes perfect on the first take. The co-directors were impressed how he immersed himself so thoroughly in the character. Miller, who has a cameo as a priest shot dead by Marv, would tell the crew 'He's going in,' whenever he spied Mickey ready to inhabit fully the brokenhearted enforcer character.

Mickey responded well to working again with Robert Rodriguez. He thought the moviemaker was incredibly cool the way he would walk around the set in cowboy hat and boots and strumming a guitar making up music for the movie's soundtrack at the same time as directing the action.

Playing the likeable vigilante in *Sin City* brought Mickey some of the best reviews he had had in a very long time and the huge success of the film (it took $120 million worldwide), which also starred Bruce Willis, Jessica Alba and Clive Owen, introduced him to a new generation of moviegoers. Mickey Rourke was hot again. He got an especially enthusiastic welcome in London from the crowds outside and the audience inside the UK première of *Sin City*, at which he sat next to Madonna and Guy Ritchie.

Mickey turned down a role in Guy Ritchie's 2005 crime film *Revolver* in order to work with director Tony Scott again in *Domino* (2005). The movie, full of dizzying fast cuts but not very involving, was based on the true story of the late Domino Harvey. The title character, played by Keira Knightley, was the daughter of film actor Laurence Harvey who left her glamorous and pampered life behind to become a gun-toting bounty hunter. Mickey plays Ed Moseby, the veteran bounty hunter who takes her under his wing and becomes a father figure. The character was based on real-life bounty hunter Ed Martinez, who served as a consultant on the film. Mickey's old mate Christopher Walken was also in the cast as a reality TV producer.

Scott had to fight to cast Mickey ahead of a flavour-of-the-month actor who was also up for the part. Mickey didn't think directors would still have to fight for him after the reports of his good behaviour on *Once Upon a Time in Mexico*, but they did and he was grateful to Tony Scott for doing so – and for having the script rewritten to beef up his part. That script, from *Donnie Darko*'s Richard Kelly, featured 123 F-words, a lot even for a Mickey Rourke movie.

Mickey hasn't always been complimentary about actresses, finding many of them needy, dumb and self-absorbed, but he was very impressed by *Domino* leading lady Keira Knightley, noting that the British actress was a real lady and very different from her Hollywood contemporaries, spending her spare time reading books, for example, rather than endlessly texting her friends. As he watched his poised 21-year-old co-star be word perfect on every take, friendly to everyone, give a convincing performance in a role which was something of a stretch for her and always turning up punctually on set, he reflected just how different his undisciplined younger self had been on previous movies.

Just before *Domino* was due to be released, 35-year-old Domino Harvey was found dead in the bathtub of her Hollywood home. The coroner later ruled that she had died from an accidental overdose of a powerful painkiller. Mickey, who had got to know her while making the movie and hit it off with the fascinating character, was hit hard by her death and attended her funeral, which he found profoundly moving. Domino never got to see the movie.

Mickey Rourke has not exactly been flooded during his career with offers to appear in family-friendly movies, so he was pleasantly surprised to find himself filming *Stormbreaker* (2006), a spy adventure aimed at kids and teens. He was also glad to be back in London, one of his favourite cities, to shoot the movie which was based on the first of a series of thrilling and big-selling books by Anthony Horowitz about a kind of junior James Bond named Alex Ryder. Newcomer Alex Pettyfer played the boy hero and was surrounded by a quality cast including Bill Nighy, Ewan McGregor, Alicia Silverstone, Andy Serkis and Stephen Fry.

Mickey played the villain Darrius Sayle, a flamboyantly dressed tycoon with an elaborate plan to take revenge on the British Prime Minister for bullying him when they were at school together by killing all of Britain's schoolchildren with a computer virus.

Stormbreaker failed to make a killing at the box office, thereby foiling plans for this to be the first in a franchise of Alex Ryder films.

There had also been high hopes for *Killshot* (2005/2009) as it was based on a novel by Elmore Leonard, many of whose stories, including *Out of Sight*, *Get Shorty* and *3.10 to Yuma*, had been turned into successful films. In a lead role originally intended for Robert De Niro when the movie was set to be made several years earlier, Mickey was cast as hit-man Armand 'The Blackbird' Degas, a menacing figure who kills anyone who sees his face. *Shakespeare in Love* director John Madden, whose perfectionist approach impressed Mickey, was behind the camera and hit-maker Harvey Weinstein was producing. With all those impressive credentials, it's surprising that *Killshot* didn't turn out too well – but instead had a long and rocky journey to the screen. After filming in 2005, and undergoing reshoots and heavy editing, the movie sat on the shelf for four years until finally being released only in five Arizona cinemas in January 2009 and coming out on DVD five months later.

Despite uneven pacing and some abrupt transitions, the film is rescued by a really good performance from Mickey as the half Native-American cool contract killer who is rattled by the death of his younger brother during an assignment. He then makes the mistake of teaming up with Richie Nix, played by Joseph Gordon Levitt, a young, loudmouth crook who reminds him of his late brother; when their first job together goes wrong, two witnesses – an estranged couple played by Diane Lane and Thomas Jane – get away and flee into FBI witness protection. Mickey's character, The Blackbird, spends the rest of the film trying to track down and kill them and the climactic shootout is breathlessly exciting.

It was rough on Mickey that after finally clawing his way to a lead role in a prestigious film, everything should all fall apart through no fault of his own and hardly anyone got to see the movie in cinemas.

Through all these setbacks, Mickey somehow kept the faith that one day a film would come along that would again enable him to show just what a brilliant actor he is and the world would sit up and notice. That day finally came when he landed the lead role in *The Wrestler* (2008). In it, he plays washed-up former wrestling star Randy 'The Ram' Robinson who now fights in small-time bouts and supplements his income with part-time supermarket work. When his health declines, he is forced to reassess his life.

There is a full chapter later on the making of the movie, and it goes on to show that the success of that film prompted a string of offers for more great roles – which is what Mickey had wanted for years. But before he knew all those exciting opportunities would be coming his way, Mickey accepted a small role in *The Informers* (2009).

This one saw Mickey playing a thoroughly unpleasant character – a psychotic kidnapper who snatches kids for a gang of paedophiles. He has less than five minutes of screen time but is creepily effective and oddly appealing as Ray-Bans- and Rolex-wearing scumbag Peter who involves a hotel doorman in his latest kidnap scheme. Playing that reluctant accomplice role was Brad Renfro, 25, the troubled former child star of *The Client* who had battled drink and drug problems for years. Mickey bonded with Brad on set, was impressed with his young co-star's talent and keen to help him get his life back on track. He invited Brad to come and stay with him in New York any time he wanted. But Renfro never took him up on the offer. Shortly after filming, the actor died of an accidental heroin overdose in January 2008, one week before Heath Ledger died from an accidental overdose of prescription medication. The movie, his last, was dedicated to Brad's memory.

The Informers was also notable for being the first time Kim Basinger and Mickey Rourke had starred in the same film since *9½ Weeks* – but they don't have any scenes together. When they met on the red carpet at the première in Los Angeles, it was the first time they had seen each other in 23 years. It was a happy reunion as Kim had sent Mickey a letter saying how much she had enjoyed *The Wrestler* and he had been so touched to receive it that reading the letter brought him to tears.

Basinger's character is the long-suffering wife of Billy Bob Thornton's Hollywood studio executive who has been cheating on her with a TV newsreader, played by Winona Ryder. Rhys Ifans, Amber Heard and Chris Isaak also appear in the sex-, drugs- and violence-filled movie, based on a Bret Easton Ellis novel, which follows a series of loosely connected characters over a week in 1983. It seemed like a promising idea but didn't engage the audience, the film was trashed by critics, its stars failed to promote it and, when the movie got shoved out into US cinemas in the last weekend of April 2009, it bombed badly at the box office.

The Informers earned a dismal total of $315,000 from 484 cinemas that opening weekend and swiftly disappeared. Only four cinemagoers showed up for the first public screening in Los Angeles – I was among them.

I've seen every movie Mickey has ever made. They've not all been good – in fact, many have been downright dreadful – but his star quality and undimmed talent has shone through in every single one.

5

Femmes Fatales

With a screech of car tyres and a flair for the dramatic entrance, Mickey Rourke rolled up in his classic 1961 black Cadillac outside the hilltop church in Palos Verdes, California, where he was to say his wedding vows.

It was 31 January 1981, the sun was shining and he looked quite a sight in a light purple suit, lavender shirt and purple tie. Minutes later, he would walk down the aisle with beautiful actress Debra Feuer, whom he had met and fallen head-over-heels in love with almost a year ago to that day.

The proud groom had planned every aspect of the wedding himself, even designing Debra's ring of diamonds and rubies, his favourite jewel.

As his most precious jewel of all – the blushing bride – came into view, Mickey thought they would stay together forever.

How wrong he was.

■　　■　　■

Until Mickey was well into his twenties, he had never had a serious relationship – and then he fell in love at first sight with dazzling Debra Feuer. They met while working on *Hardcase*, a one-off TV crime drama in which he played a criminal and she was the undercover cop out to arrest him.

Between scenes, Mickey's eyes were mostly on Debra rather than his script. He would stare longingly at her and then quickly look away whenever she caught him gazing over.

Feuer, barely 21 at the time, felt Mickey was shy and strange – but she was certainly attracted by his acting talent. She admired how he read his lines so truthfully but without effort.

When the camera rolled, the awkward young man came to life and gave a combustible performance that reminded Debra of her acting idol, Marlon Brando. She invited him out to dinner at an Italian restaurant, purely as friends, one actor to another, but started falling for Mickey as soon as they began to talk. Neither of them touched their food. He described an idea for a boxing movie he wanted to make called *Homeboy* and she listened spellbound. The attraction came as a surprise to her because he just wasn't her type – she normally only fancied Latin men.

Debra also admitted later in several press interviews that she found it surprising that Mickey hadn't tried to kiss her on their first date. He was probably just nervous because she had made a massive impression on him. Mickey knew that night that he wanted to marry Debra.

He proposed just a few months later, she said no, but he kept on popping the question and getting knock-backs. Debra didn't want to get married as she was focused on her career and, as they continued to date, she asked him to slow things down.

But she was young and in love and, when a love-sick Mickey gave her an ultimatum that she had to marry him or he would never see her again, she relented and accepted the proposal. By the time they were married, Mickey was on the verge of the big time having made *Body Heat*, he was about to film *Diner* and had started to get some high-paying movie offers coming his way.

The newlyweds bought a house in the Hollywood Hills and settled down to married life. Neither of them wanted children at that stage – Mickey's own turbulent childhood had completely put him off the idea of fatherhood – and they seemed perfectly happy with each other . . . at least at first. But it soon became clear they didn't have much in common. She liked to go out early and be in bed before it got too late. But Mickey was a night owl who didn't ever like to go out until midnight.

When *Diner* came out, became relatively successful and brought him a head-turning first taste of fame, their relationship quickly soured. They had rows – largely over all the time Mickey was spending out with his mates rather than staying home with his wife. When she called him up at the Beverly Hills office where he spent a great deal of time hanging out with his pals, Mickey would tell them, 'It's my old lady,' a nickname which infuriated and humiliated Debra. She would also complain about his extravagance – as soon as he got a lot of cash together, Mickey splashed out on expensive cars and his first Harley Davidson motorbike.

As the next few years went by and Mickey became more

and more successful, Debra watched her husband change into a self-destructive star. There was always some drama going on in his career, such as his clashes with authority figures, which Debra attributed in later interviews to his rage at his stepfather. But there was drama at home, too.

Mickey was a jealous and controlling husband. He didn't want her to work but wanted Debra at his side all the time. He would intimidate other actors if he believed they were paying her too much attention. Willem Defoe was one who felt Mickey's wrath as he worked with Debra on the crime thriller *To Live and Die in LA*, in which she played the villain's girlfriend.

Mickey's eccentric behaviour started to show itself. He was riddled with phobias. For example, he wouldn't go in the sea because he was frightened a shark would get him.

Debra believes all that insecurity led him to the bad behaviour which became a hallmark of his Hollywood career.

Mickey suddenly became very opinionated about show-business and inflicted his views and his demands on his wife. He would see her working with actors and producers whom he didn't rate – and it really annoyed him. Mickey failed to share her idealistic, romantic view of Hollywood, seeing it instead as a giant pool of sharks.

Debra felt stardom eventually went to his head and that it left Mickey very cynical, sour and disillusioned with the movie world. There were plenty of arguments and temper tantrums which hurt the relationship.

Mickey had an old-fashioned view of marriage, in which he wanted his wife to play second fiddle to her husband rather than having her own ambitions – but Debra just wasn't that kind of person. She wasn't at all pleased. For example, during the period when he was preparing for and making *9½ Weeks*, Mickey got into character by isolating himself from her – going to live in a hotel suite and leaving her home alone – and becoming selfish rather than sensitive to her needs. The movie made him a superstar but his wife's mood wasn't helped by the fact that her own acting career was failing to catch fire.

The marriage really got into trouble as Mickey started to be seen out with other women, including model-actress Lauren Hutton who was in a car crash with the actor in his Mercedes as Debra waited up for Mickey to come home. They had been driving on the twisting Mulholland Drive in LA with Hutton at the wheel when she suddenly lost control and crashed into a mountainside. Neither of them was hurt but the car was written off. Mickey took Lauren with him to buy a new one the next day – and he was at the wheel this time when they drove away from the Mercedes dealership. Despite his womanising image, Debra doesn't believe Mickey ever cheated on her. But he did seem to lose all interest in their marriage as he just wasn't around – and refused to try couples therapy.

Mickey seemed to prefer living in hotels to living at home and Debra rarely visited him on film sets, choosing instead to practise yoga and meditation. They starred together in the movie *Homeboy* while they were estranged, but working together failed to bring Mickey and Debra back together as a couple. She filed for divorce in 1989 and the split was made final a year later.

Mickey felt bad about giving up on the marriage and how he had treated Debra and although she only asked for her fair share in the split, he gave her everything. While she stayed in the marital home, he bought a new place 15 miles away.

Debra Feuer's movie career never took off in the way that her husband's did, but her relationship with Mickey improved over the years and they are now close friends. Debra is currently a yoga teacher and has married again – to cameraman Scott Fuller. When she fell for Scott, Mickey insisted on meeting him so he could give her new man the seal of approval – which he did. He likes Scott and the couple's 10-year-old daughter Jessica Ruby. She calls him Uncle Mickey and he invites her round to play with his dogs. And when he finished filming *The Wrestler*, one of Mickey's first calls was to Debra, excitedly telling her he had just given the performance of his life.

After splitting from Debra, Mickey wasn't single for long. He fell hard for Terry Farrell, an up-and-coming actress who had been in a soap opera called *Paper Dolls* and who would later go on to find fame as Jadzia Dax in the TV series *Star Trek: Deep Space Nine*.

Much like the marriage he had just left, this, too, was a stormy relationship with many bust-ups. But making up was the best part – and how they enjoyed it. They were a passionate couple who would disappear into the bedroom for hours on end. If Mickey looked tired a lot in this period, it was likely due to his marathon sex sessions with his girlfriend. Tactile Terry was always touching him, even when he was talking business with someone. People who saw them together remember her sitting at his feet or standing close to him, mouthing the words, 'I love you.'

But in case his legions of female fans would be upset to

find he had a steady girlfriend, Mickey didn't advertise the fact they were dating. He would avoid being photographed with her when out in public and didn't mention Terry in interviews. The romance only really went public when it ended. Eventually, the increasing number of arguments got too much for Terry and she ended their romance in a phone call. Mickey was in Italy at the time and just about to make a live appearance on a TV chat show. Minutes later, millions of Italian viewers watched stunned as the star guest broke down in tears on air saying how much he needed Terry and couldn't live without her. The couple did give it another try a short time afterwards but couldn't patch things up and split for good.

Mickey was romantically linked with several other women after that, including Princess Stephanie of Monaco, but that relationship never developed because Mickey didn't like the way the royal so often wanted to be the centre of attention.

But he was soon to find a lesser-known beauty whom he would treat like a princess.

Carré Otis, a young model whose stunning face adorned covers of glossy fashion magazines like *Vogue*, *Elle*, *Harper's* and *Cosmopolitan*, as well as ads for Guess and Calvin Klein, was cast as Mickey's lover in the erotic movie *Wild Orchid* – and the pair fell for each other on and off screen.

It was a part she so nearly missed out on as bigger names were offered it first. Brooke Shields was first choice for the role of young innocent Emily Reed but that failed to work out after Brooke made it clear that she was not prepared to do the nude scenes. Supermodel Cindy Crawford, who was looking to break into movies, was then offered the role but eventually turned it down, deciding she didn't want such explicit sex scenes to be part of her first film. So in stepped Carré for her film début. She may have lacked acting experience but her looks certainly weren't lacking.

Carré and Mickey fell for each other on day one – and it was an intense attraction from the start. With his divorce from Debra now finalised and the Terry heartbreak behind him, Mickey went all out to woo Carré and she seemed equally wild about him. The stunner from San Francisco loved the actor's strength, intelligence, professionalism and looks. Meanwhile, Mickey was utterly smitten, calling his co-star, 'One of the most beautiful women God ever created.'

When the pair shared an intense sex scene in the movie, there were many who believed they weren't faking it but actually made love for real on camera . . . a claim Carré later denied. Their romance didn't fizzle out after filming ended. Instead, their feelings for each other grew even stronger and, when Mickey proposed, Carré eagerly said, 'Yes.'

It seemed like a fairytale – the movie star marrying the supermodel. The lovebirds were married on 26 June 1992 in beautiful Big Sur, California, and then had an idyllic honeymoon, taking off together on a romantic road trip, driving across America in his 1969 Road Runner convertible.

However, the honeymoon was soon over and the stormy years of marriage began. Both of them had equally explosive personalities – they were like thunder and lightning together – and frequent clashes resulted. Mickey wanted his wife to give up or scale down her modelling work despite the fact that she had some big money contracts lined up, and that was something she was happy to do in order to spend more time with her husband.

Theirs was a passionate relationship in every way and the pair were so devoted they each had the other's name tattooed on their skin. But the tempestuous couple also generated plenty of ink in the tabloids. Their six-year marriage would be full of headline-hitting allegations of drug abuse and violence.

The first shocker came on 22 September 1991 when, while visiting Mickey in Sante Fe, New Mexico, where he was filming *White Sands*, Carré was shot by a gun registered to Mickey. She was rushed to hospital with a bullet wound in her shoulder and the police were called. Carré told the cops that her husband didn't shoot her and it had all been an accident – she had moved a black bag which, unknown to her, contained a loaded .357 Magnum and it accidentally went off. No charges were filed.

High drama like this was nothing new to Carré who came from a damaged background – she has said both of her parents had drink problems, her first boyfriend was drug-addled and she started using booze and drugs herself at an early age, while also battling anorexia and self-esteem problems. Carré left home at 15 and moved to New York to model where her extreme dieting and drug use would gradually do her so much damage that she ended up needing heart surgery by the time she was 30.

Carré has openly admitted being a longtime heroin addict and Mickey spent a great deal of time attempting to get her off the drug. Those widely reported attempts ranged from booking her into a special clinic to beating up the drug pushers who were feeding his wife's habit. When laying into one of them, he apparently hit the guy so hard that his attack sent a stream of blood gushing high into the air.

But it was for allegedly hitting Carré that he found himself carted off by police on 18 July 1994. Mickey was arrested for 'misdemeanour spousal battery', and was accused of kicking, slapping and knocking down his wife during a chance encounter at the Los Angeles office of their publicist. He pleaded not guilty to the charge, which carried a maximum one-year jail sentence.

Mickey's mugshot was picked up by media outlets around the world. The actor was ordered to stand trial but the charge was eventually dismissed in December after Otis had failed to show up for two court appearances when she was due to testify. 'We had been attempting for several weeks to contact her through her attorney and were unable to locate her,' said Mike Qualls, spokesman for the Los Angeles City Attorney's Office.

She and Mickey had separated after the incident and he was banned from her fashion shows for a while – it looked all over for the couple. But on Valentine's Day 1995, they announced they were reunited and Carré moved back in with Mickey.

They tried to rediscover the magic and romance – and even made a second film together, the poorly received and little seen 1996 'thriller' *Exit in Red*. But the new beginning didn't work out and, after the dramas and disappointment all became too much, Carré left Mickey for good.

Mickey found it impossible to cope without the love of his life. He felt suicidal and was at one point held for observation for 29 hours at an LA hospital. There was also the incident in the church when the kindly priest talked him out of his plan to shoot Carré's violent drug pusher then turn the gun on himself.

Mickey tried to change his ways so Carré would come back to him, and started therapy as part of the plan to become a better person. In total, he waited nearly 10 years for his beloved Carré to come back to him – but she never did. She moved on. They continued to speak from time to time but it just wasn't the same between them.

Carré happily conquered her drug problem and became a great deal healthier, not only with 12-step-style recovery methods, running and yoga, but also by becoming interested in Buddhism, going on retreats, doing voluntary work delivering medical supplies in Nepal and generally having a spiritual awakening that helped her kick the drug habit. She put on a considerable amount of weight – but then re-invented herself as a plus-size model. Carré next tried to inspire others by sharing her recovery story on college campuses, lecturing about addiction, spousal abuse and body image. Carré Otis is now away from the spotlight, happily living the quiet life in Mill Valley, California, with a new family. She has a second husband now, Matthew, an environmental scientist whom she married in December 2005, seven months after meeting him while out hiking. The couple have a daughter, Jade, born on 11 November 2006. The baby was a wonderful surprise as Carré hadn't had a period in six years and had been told she would never get pregnant.

As for Mickey, no woman has come along since Carré to replace the gaping hole she left in his life. In all the years since she left him, he has never had dinner twice with the same girl in a week. But Mickey has had a string of one-night stands both at home and on his travels around the world. Over the years, he has taken a procession of women back to his room at Blakes Hotel, where he stays whenever he is in London, or his homes in America.

But Mickey hasn't had a steady girlfriend for a long, long time, shares his feelings with no one but his therapist and his priest, and shares his bed most nights with his pet dogs.

He continues to be a flirt, though. Appearing on BBC TV's *The Graham Norton Show* in October 2008, he kept making cheeky advances, on air, to fellow guest Jessica Biel and asked if she was married – seemingly not realising her boyfriend was one of the world's leading heart-throbs, Justin Timberlake.

At a December 2008 public Q&A in Santa Monica, California, during a festival of Mickey Rourke films, he responded to a question about *The Wrestler* from a pretty girl in the audience by saying, 'Look at you, you're not ugly. You know, there are things I like better than making movies . . .'

In late January 2009, Mickey hooked up with Chinese-American actress Bai Ling.

He was at Hollywood celebrity hotspot the Chateau Marmont Hotel with Sean Penn when he was approached by the skinny beauty. They had briefly met before when she attended *The Wrestler* LA première after-party a month earlier. Soon, they were all over each other and a brief romance blossomed in the following days. One thing they bonded over was their love of animals. Mickey loves his dogs while Bai dotes on her cat Qiji.

But that relationship, like so many of his others, ran aground just a few days later.

The next famous face he was romantically linked with was Courtney Love – after they both won prizes at the *Elle* Style Awards in London in February 2009. But Mickey was quick to shoot down reports of a romance with Kurt Cobain's widow, saying, rather harshly, 'I'd rather be on a deserted island with a gorilla!' At the same London event, Mickey had admired married British actress Thandi Newton and told her, 'You're fit.'

Days earlier at the BAFTA Film Awards after-show party, Mickey renewed his acquaintance with sexy blonde Abi Titmuss, whom he had met two years earlier at a music festival. The 32-year-old – famous for a taped sex and drugs scandal – was among the guests at the Grosvenor House Hotel bash and later claimed to the British press that Mickey had propositioned her at the event but she had refused to sleep with him.

Meanwhile, back in Hollywood, someone also distancing herself from Mickey was the young actress who plays his daughter in *The Wrestler*, Evan Rachel Wood. The 21-year-old spoke out firmly to dispel growing rumours that she was dating Mickey, saying, 'I'm not attracted to him. He's too old for me. Nothing ever happened and nothing ever will.'

But rumours about Mickey's love life were constantly fuelled by potential liaisons with a variety of high-profile women. On his return to the States, Mickey hung out with Paris Hilton at her 28th birthday party, but the night after that he was arm in arm and out on the town in New York with German model Manon von Gerkan, the former girlfriend of illusionist David Blaine. Then when he went to Moscow in March 2009 to research his role as a Russian

Young, handsome and full of potential, Mickey Rourke burst onto the Hollywood scene looking like a superstar in the making. *(Corbis)*

Rourke's mannered, mumbling and mesmeric performance in *Rumble Fish* marked him out as a real talent to watch. *(Rex Features)*

A rare picture of Mickey with his former girlfriend Terry Farrell. Theirs was a lusty, low profile, high intensity but doomed relationship.

A scene from the atmospheric, acclaimed and haunting thriller *Angel Heart* which is widely considered to feature the definitive Mickey Rourke screen performance. *(Rex Features)*

Mickey with Kim Basinger in a scene from *9 ½ Weeks*, the erotic classic which made them both sex symbols. But their relationship wasn't nearly as sizzling off camera. *(Rex Features)*

Mickey with his ex-wife Carre Otis. Their rollercoaster relationship was passionate, stormy, headline hitting and ultimately heartbreaking. *(Getty Images)*

The poster for Mickey's first fight as a professional boxer in May 1991. 'Marielito' was the star attraction of a five fight card in Fort Lauderdale, Florida. His autographed message on it shows he was better at boxing than spelling. He wrote: 'It's never to late if your willing to pay the pipper.'

Mickey is declared the winner of that debut fight against Steve Powell. Boxing was back in his blood now and all thoughts of this being a one-off were abandoned as he embarked on a new career as a professional fighter.
(Getty Images)

Mickey leaps back into the big time as *The Wrestler*. His remarkable performance as Randy the Ram Robinson reminded Hollywood of his great talent and won him both awards and a great deal of respect. *(Rex Features)*

Psychologist Dr Yvonne Thomas who provides her professional analysis of Mickey Rourke in this book.
(Harry Langdon)

Rourke's former hairstylist Teddy Antolin who prepared Mickey for photo shoots: 'He always looked at polaroids taken during his film shoots.'

Mickey Rourke demonstrates cowboy cool while being interviewed by GMTV Hollywood correspondent Carla Romano at the 2009 *Vanity Fair* Oscar party just a couple of hours after missing out on the Best Actor Oscar.

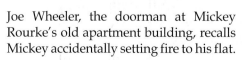

Leading Los Angeles fitness trainer Joe Rivera befriended Mickey: 'A sweetheart of a guy but also a tough cookie and a troubled soul.'

Joe Wheeler, the doorman at Mickey Rourke's old apartment building, recalls Mickey accidentally setting fire to his flat.

Comeback king Mickey Rourke shows off his Golden Globe best actor award for *The Wrestler*, a triumph which made him the toast of Hollywood again. *(Corbis)*

villain in *Iron Man 2*, Mickey was in the glamorous company of Russian boxer-turned-pop star Irson Kudikova. Then in May, he was passionately snogging a 24-year-old Victoria's Secret model, Eugenie Voldona, in the middle of a New York nightclub. Eleven years after his divorce from Carré Otis, he clearly hasn't lost his lust for models.

Mickey has always had an eye for the ladies and knows what he is looking for. Asked about his taste in women, he once said, 'It's like what I look for in a horse . . . I don't want a thick neck and short legs.'

It seems he has now settled down to life as a swinging bachelor and Mickey boasts that he currently gets laid more often than he did in his late-1980s heyday. And that is despite, or perhaps because of, his favourite chat-up line, which apparently works surprisingly well. Having spotted a girl he fancies, Mickey has been known to say, 'I can take you home and fuck you until you go crazy.'

6

Sin Citizen

Mickey felt on top of the world late in the evening of 9 November 2008 as he strolled along Sunset Boulevard on his way into hip Hollywood nightclub Hyde while having his picture taken by an eager crowd of paparazzi photographers. The media had largely ignored Mickey for many years but now he was relishing being back in the spotlight thanks to his comeback role in acclaimed new movie *The Wrestler*.

In interviews promoting the film over the previous few days, he had been insisting that the bad-boy antics and temper explosions of the past were behind him and now he was a changed man. But it only took one question from the press pack that night to end the serenity and bring out his anger and sharp tongue once more. When asked about a recent article that claimed he was dating young actress Evan Rachel Wood, who played his daughter in *The Wrestler*, Mickey denied it and then made a nasty statement that suggested he still had some way to go to bring his demons under control. He snapped, 'Tell that faggot who wrote that shit that I'd like to break his fucking legs.'

It was a case of chivalry gone wrong but, like many times before, Mickey's big mouth had got him in trouble.

■　■　■

Mickey may not have won an Oscar, at least not yet, but if there was a prize for craziest behaviour by any living actor, he would have few rivals. For despite his undoubted talent, Mickey has spent a lot of time acting more like an arsehole than an actor. He has been the subject of more eccentric behaviour stories than any Hollywood star since Marlon Brando.

Despite rumours to the contrary, booze and drugs have never been his big problem – it's his anger and his attitude which have most often let him down. The Incredible Hulk kept his temper better than Mickey Rourke, an emotional time bomb who spent many years rebelling against figures in authority and has never liked people telling him what to do ever since his domineering stepfather came into his life.

He would have been a much bigger name in Hollywood if only he had taken the advice of various representatives, directors and producers who lined up some amazing star-making parts for him. Mickey turned down lead roles in some of the biggest films of the 1980s – *Beverly Hills Cop*, *Top Gun*, *Highlander*, *Rain Man*, *48 Hours*, *The Untouchables* and *Platoon* – and in the 1990s he rejected supporting roles in blockbusters such as *The Silence of the Lambs* and *Pulp Fiction*. He stubbornly chose to turn down hero roles and instead went his own way, building a career largely playing the only kind of parts that interested him – dark, edgy and dangerous characters, outlaws and various other bad boys.

It was a role he was playing all too frequently in real life as well – going around with a chip on his shoulder and seemingly also carrying an edge of danger. Hollywood executives were scared of him for the way he used to show up on set with an entourage of Hell's Angels, bodyguards and various other tattooed tough guys. In fact, Mickey always seemed to have a pack of human rottweilers with him. Growing up around gang members and boxers in Miami had instilled in him an admiration for hard men like these and he felt a lot more comfortable in their company than around actors or studio 'suits'.

Many of these minders were on his payroll at up to $1,000 a week but, because Mickey wasn't being attacked by demonic stalkers or drug-crazed louts every minute, they mostly earned their money by fetching his cigarettes and projecting an unapproachable image.

Mickey was nothing but generous to the flunkies in his circle. In addition to the high wages, he even bought them motorbikes and cars. But he created a menacing picture to the outside world.

When he walked into a restaurant, all macho attitude and tough guy swagger, people would flinch as if antici-pating trouble. Neighbours in swanky Beverly Hills would be horrified by the noise and party atmosphere at his mansion which would regularly have more than twenty motorbikes parked outside – Mickey's six Harley Davidsons, five belonging to his brother Joey, who lived in the guest house and flew a Jolly Roger pirate flag outside, and ten or so more belonging to visiting biker pals. Actor Richard Harris, who lived there before him, had warned Mickey that the neighbours wouldn't welcome him with open arms, but Mickey wasn't going to change his ways and saw it as their problem. Unsurprisingly, the neighbours on either side of him moved out.

Outraged Beverly Hills council members and residents demanded the closure of Mickey and Joey's, the tiny street-side café he co-owned in the heart of the city's swanky shopping district, because he was using the posh street outside for noisy, night-time, high-speed Harley Davidson races with his leather-clad mates. It was also claimed that the presence of beer-swilling, unshaven, tattooed types in sleeveless t-shirts around the stand unsettled shoppers and frightened children visiting Le Grand Passage, the up-market arcade of shops where it was located. Beverly Hills cops even impounded his Harley in the summer of 1989 on a 'muffler violation' – basically saying it was making too much noise.

Mickey's bad reputation grew as he reportedly developed social contacts with gangland figures and even showed up at a Brooklyn court to watch the 1992 murder and racketeering trial of Mafioso John Gotti, saying he was supporting his friend. Mickey had previously met Gotti while researching a project and said he had been very generous with his time and insight. Suddenly, Mickey had gone from being the next James Dean to the new George Raft, a previous era's hot actor who had turned down star-making parts, took many tough guy roles and associated with mobsters.

Mickey certainly had more time for Mob bosses than movie bosses. In the 1980s, he mounted a brass plaque on the front door of his trailer which read, 'All studio executives and producers to stay the fuck away.'

Meanwhile, Mickey was just too flash for a lot of people's tastes, driving around in a gold-plated Rolls-Royce, the purchase of which was inspired by his Elvis obsession.

Timekeeping was another problem for Mickey and he missed early-morning calls to film sets because he had been out partying all night. To stop that repeatedly happening on *9½ Weeks*, director Adrian Lyne posted a minder outside his door to stop him going out late and to make sure he got to work on time.

At the height of his stardom, Mickey was so irresponsible that he couldn't even remember his agent's name. He would call up his agency of the time, CAA, and ask the receptionist, 'Who's the little bald guy with the white Porsche?'

Mickey has offended plenty of Hollywood colleagues with outspoken comments, including Mel Gibson who publicly disagreed when Mickey claimed that acting wasn't a man's job. Mel said, 'Mickey just thinks he is a tough guy in a black t-shirt.' Mickey replied, 'Mel's problem is that I am.'

After the LA riots of 1992, Mickey told an interviewer that the films of director Spike Lee were partly responsible for the violent uprising. He was quoted as saying, 'The blood of Los Angeles falls on those who instigated this revolt – the malicious prophets of black cinema and rap music, the movies such as those of Spike Lee and John Singleton.'

Do the Right Thing director Spike Lee responded, 'Mickey Rourke is a fucking asshole. He's a fucking redneck, motherfucking cracker. I mean, he's an idiot. He's been riding a motorcycle without a helmet and he's punch drunk from being in the ring. How can Mickey Rourke say that me and John Singleton are responsible for the riots in LA? Like his films are responsible? He should get a fucking shave and take a shower.' Actress Whoopi Goldberg also weighed in on the war of words, saying, 'I think Mickey has taken a few too may lefts to the head.'

In 2006, Mickey was reported to have raged against Tom Cruise, calling him a 'cunt' following the A–lister's pro-nouncements against therapy. In TV interviews, the superstar had opposed psychiatry, as does his religion, the Church of Scientology, which has historically been at odds with the established medical and mental health community. Mickey had been in therapy for years, credits it with helping him make a comeback, and his one word response made it clear what he thought of Cruise's argument.

Barfly director Barbet Schroeder was so disgusted when Mickey suddenly dropped out, without explanation, of another film they had been developing that he put a note on the actor's front door saying he would never speak to him again – and he hasn't.

Outspoken Mickey has tended to say what he feels, regardless of the consequences. It meant he had no problem breaking the unwritten actor's rule that you never slag off your own films. For example, he called *Harley Davidson and the Marlboro Man*, 'a complete piece of shit'. And he's happy to say exactly what he thinks to people's faces rather than behind their backs. He told the writer of *Harley Davidson and the Marlboro Man*, Don Michael Paul, in no uncertain terms just how bad he thought his script was and then told him to fuck off.

Rock stars are more known for smashing up hotel rooms than movie actors but Mickey appears to have done his bit to change that. Tycoon Donald Trump, owner of New York's posh Plaza Hotel, claimed the star caused $20,000 worth of damage to his suite during a 1994 stay and the room had to be closed to guests for a while during which extensive repairs were carried out.

The Tinseltown terror's behaviour became so laughably bad that Mickey eventually became a punchline for comedians and writers. American humourist Joe Queenan wrote a memorable article, which quickly inspired a spin-off TV special, in which he became Mickey Rourke for a day – dressing, speaking and smoking in true Rourke style, and fucking with people like, well, you get the picture. He grunged up for the assignment by abstaining from bathing, shaving or washing his hair for seven days beforehand. By the time his Rourke wildness was over, he had smoked 82 Marlboro cigarettes, threatened journalists with physical harm, sneered and snarled at passers-by and blindfolded a female friend, *9½ Weeks*-style, before force-feeding her the contents of his fridge.

His history of explosive incidents have made Mickey a gift to journalists who have chronicled his career. But he hasn't always been so nice to them either. Mickey has undoubtedly become much better in his relations with the media recently – actually giving considered, honest and emotional answers to questions – but it wasn't like that in the bad old days. There were many incidents around the world where he was dismissive of his promotional responsibilities. One typical example concerns an incident occurring around 20 years before a triumphant visit to Italy promoting *The Wrestler* at the Venice Film Festival. Two decades earlier, he had left the same event with insults ringing in his ears. It all followed a moody press conference performance. First, he wouldn't speak into the microphone, then he got his translator to answer the questions for him because he couldn't be bothered to reply himself.

Outraged by this insult, one of the Italian journalists stood up to complain then walked out, urging all the other reporters in the room to do the same. He was applauded wildly but only six journalists followed him out of the room.

Mickey was also supposed to be doing telephone interviews during his 48 hours in Venice but wrecked that plan by taking the phone in his room off the hook. He left Venice quickly by boat, leaving photographers fuming at the waterfront that he hadn't given them enough time posing for pictures. As Mickey sped away, several of the Italian snappers shouted after him, '*Stronzo*!' meaning 'You piece of crap!'

Mickey also disgusted reporters at the 1989 Deauville Film Festival by starting his press conference 20 minutes late, ending it 40 minutes early and saying very little in between.

But it wasn't just members of the press and the Hollywood establishment of whom he had fallen foul over the years – Mickey also got into trouble with the law.

The arrest which grabbed the most headlines was the alleged battery of wife Carré Otis, for which the charges were dropped after she chose not to testify. Mickey also spent a few hours behind bars in January 1994 following an argument which erupted after he helped bouncers throw some unruly customers out of Mickey's, a Miami nightspot to which he had lent his name, status and regular presence. He ended up in a shouting match with one of the ejected customers, a large, riled-up crowd outside and also with the police, who arrested him for resisting arrest – a charge later dropped. The irate film star later said in a press conference that someone had bad-mouthed him that night. He explained, 'If somebody says "Suck my dick" to me, yeah, I'm gonna get really mad and I'm gonna be offended by it. But I did not hit the individual and I did not touch him.' The club's name was soon afterwards changed to XTC, apparently because Mickey's name didn't draw sufficient punters.

He was arrested again in Miami in 2007 on suspicion of driving a motor scooter while intoxicated, a charge later reduced to reckless driving and which, ultimately, went away.

Mickey, who had been clubbing at hot spot Mansion, was pulled over at 4.11am when his new green Vespa, carrying a sexy passenger on the back, allegedly made a U-turn on a red light and swerved in front of a police car. According to the police report, he started swearing when he was stopped.

Mickey's big mouth has often got him into trouble. It is a failing which has cost him work and hurt his reputation. Speaking up and asking for his dog to get a part alongside him in the 2000 crime movie *Luck of the Draw* led to Mickey getting fired from the movie and made him a laughing stock in the film world. It all started during a discussion over his death scene. Mickey's character was supposed to walk into a warehouse, listen to dialogue between co-stars Eric Roberts, Ice-T and Dennis Hopper, and then get shot. But he wanted an activity to do in the scene so he wouldn't just be standing around. So he suggested to the director,

Luca Bercovici, that he should be carrying or stroking his pet chihuahua, Beau Jack. They rehearsed it like that a couple of times only for Bercovici to tell Mickey it shouldn't be done that way after all as the producer didn't want a dog in the scene. Mickey made his objections clear and they broke for lunch. Shortly afterwards, Mickey was let go, apparently for being difficult to work with, and was swiftly replaced by Michael Madsen.

It was a low point in Mickey's career, but there had been a much worse occasion two decades earlier when his outspoken ways had made him, for a time, the most hated man in Britain. He just couldn't keep his mouth shut about his delight in being cast to play an IRA gunman in the movie *A Prayer for the Dying* and made some ill-advised statements that were interpreted as expressing sympathy for the Irish Republican Army's cause.

Just before the film's release in 1987, he issued a further statement including the following words, 'As a concerned Irish-American Catholic, I wholeheartedly support the Troops Out movement and all efforts designed to assure equal human and civil rights for all citizens of Northern Ireland. There is no place in Ireland for British troops or second-class citizens.'

The comments were especially insensitive as feelings were running extra high that same year following relentless IRA violence, including more murders of British troops and the Remembrance Sunday bomb which killed 11 of the civilians who had gathered at the cenotaph in Enniskillen, Northern Ireland, to pay their respects to the war dead.

With his grandparents coming from Cork, Mickey had long been interested in the Irish Troubles and had very definite ideas about the economic and sectarian problems which would have motivated his movie character to pick up a gun and join the Provos. His research for the film had included reading a biography of IRA hunger-striker Bobby Sands and going on a two-day fact-finding mission to Belfast – during which he stayed at the most exclusive hotel in the city.

Mickey claimed to have met IRA members who had helped him better understand the Northern Ireland situation and said after his visit, 'I learned about the problem – how the Catholic minority's civil rights get stomped on like the blacks in America. How little boys see their grandfathers unable to get work because of their religion. I saw the graveyards filled with guys who died at 18, 20 or 22.'

Meanwhile, he was said to be surprised to find there were a million Unionists in Northern Ireland as he had assumed everyone there was fighting to get the British out. *A Prayer for the Dying* had been due to open the 1987 London Film Festival but was withdrawn from the event due to ongoing real-life IRA atrocities. When it did open, the film flopped at the box office.

Clearly, Mickey had little grasp of the real situation in Northern Ireland but it didn't stop him speaking out anyway because he felt so passionately about the subject. Despite all the controversy caused that time, he foolishly returned to the theme two years later – and got in even more trouble. At the 1989 Cannes Film Festival press conference to promote his role as St Francis of Assisi in the film *Francesco*, Mickey was asked if he was aware that Margaret Thatcher had quoted St Francis when she was first elected British Prime Minister in 1979. He replied, 'I really don't give a fuck what she has to say. Mrs Thatcher should have given in to the hunger-strikers of Northern Ireland.'

Then he let slip that he had given away a percentage of his fee for *Francesco* to 'certain causes in Northern Ireland'. Pressed by the British reporters to say exactly what those causes were, he made a vague mention of a fund for Joe Doherty, a notorious IRA gunman who had been convicted of murdering SAS captain Herbert Westmacott but escaped to the United States where he was currently fighting extradition back to Britain for completion of his life sentence.

The British press naturally had a field day with the naming of Mickey as one of Doherty's high-profile supporters and, the next morning, headlines such as 'YOU VILE BRAT' were screaming out from newsstands from Penzance to Perth. Incensed Conservative Member of Parliament Harry Greenway led calls for Mickey to be banned from visiting the UK ever again. Fellow Tory MP Ivor Stanbrook raged, 'His statement in Cannes is proof that Mickey is helping to finance the IRA.'

The Home Office had to answer the growing clamour for action against the movie star by stating it had no power to ban him under the Prevention of Terrorism Act unless the money had actually changed hands in Britain. Mickey was stunned by the outcry as he hadn't given any money to terrorists – but only clarified his remarks after he had been buried under a torrent of criticism. In a bid to calm the fury, he issued a statement saying, 'My remarks were an emotional response, a little confused and certainly misunderstood. I have never given funds to the IRA, Joe Doherty or anyone connected with the IRA and have no intention of doing so in the future. It is my desire to assist charitable organisations who provide help to the children who are innocent victims of the circumstances in Northern Ireland.'

His manager and spokesperson of the time, Jane Katchmer, explained that Mickey had never spoken to Doherty but received some correspondence from him about charities that help poor and homeless people and Mickey had asked her to check out whether or not they were legitimate. When he arrived in Cannes, he thought she had done that and the money had been sent – while, in actual fact, she was still looking into it. She said Mickey had wanted to support groups that take children from the fighting areas to the United States on holiday and show them there are better alternatives in life than picking up a gun. Now, if he had just said that, he wouldn't have put his career and reputation at risk. But that's Mickey Rourke for you – he lives on the edge.

Mickey vowed never to spout off against politics again but couldn't help himself during George W. Bush's final year in the White House. Mickey was one of the few celebrities to speak up for the unpopular, outgoing US President and said he felt he had done a great job. Just ahead of the November 2008 election, he said how much he admired controversial Vice-Presidential candidate Sarah Palin for her plain-speaking ways.

It was just days after the election that he used the word 'faggot' as an insulting term against that reporter who had written a critical story about him.

Even though he later apologised for his behaviour,

Mickey picked a lousy time to upset the gay community, for the homophobia debate was raging around California that month as the State's electorate had just controversially voted against gay marriage. A few months earlier, TV actor Isaiah Washington had lost his job on *Grey's Anatomy* by using the same gay slur to characterise one of his co-stars and his career has struggled to hit the heights since. Adding to the lack of sensitivity was the fact that Mickey was in an Oscar campaign against an actor playing a champion of gay rights – Sean Penn as Harvey Milk.

Things got worse for Mickey when reports emerged of him supposedly sending a leaked text message trashing Penn's performance in the film *Milk* and calling him 'one of the most homophobic people I know'. It seemed unlikely as the pair are pals and Mickey had praised Penn's performance in a newspaper interview at the time. Mickey's publicist went into fire-fighting mode, insisting, 'There is no Oscar feud between Mickey and Sean. They have known each other and been friends for a very long time. Mickey attended the New York première of *Milk* to support Sean and only has the greatest respect for him.' She did not directly call the text a fake but offered instead that 'Mickey is completely unaware of the text'.

Mickey called up Penn after the story broke to try and explain the situation but Sean said he hadn't read it, didn't want to do so and it didn't matter anyway. They remain on good terms.

Mickey needed to be on his best behaviour in the run-up to the Oscars as it is well known in Hollywood that conservative Academy voters don't always fill in their ballots based on who gave the best performance but also consider how the front-runners conduct themselves off screen. A profanity-laden speech at the BAFTA Awards and other unfortunate public comments didn't help his cause and may well have cost Mickey some crucial votes.

But he was still making controversial statements after the Oscars, issuing a threat to US TV show host Joe McHale for making a joke on his show, *The Soup*, about Mickey's late dog, Loki. Mickey's considered response was, 'That motherfucker is going to get a slap in the face.'

Despite the occasional outburst, Mickey is doing better. For one thing, he no longer associates with the same rough-and-ready characters who used to make up his entourage. Neither does he travel with a bodyguard any more. He still has the odd inebriated night out now and again – like the time in June 2009 when he staggered out of West Hollywood club Guys and Dolls and had to lean against the nearest tree for a while before locating his taxi – but that's all part of the fun.

But he's certainly no wild thing these days. Certainly, the Mickey Rourke I have met is more pussycat than mad dog. And the actor himself would argue that the troublemaker reputation which has followed him for years is largely undeserved. After all, unlike various other badly behaved Hollywood stars, Mickey Rourke has never punched out a photographer, spat on a reporter or beaten up another actor . . . and he's certainly never killed anyone.

Now a largely reformed character after many years in therapy, Mickey recognises he was his own worst enemy for many years. Largely ashamed by those mistakes, the ex-wildman takes full responsibility for the hell he raised and the enemies he made. And in several interviews, Mickey has returned to the same basic theme: 'I have nobody else to blame except Mickey Rourke.'

7

Desperate Hours

As Mickey sat in the kitchen of his LA home drinking coffee and talking softly with his brother Joey's nurse, he was having to face the devastating fact that his brave sibling was about to lose his long fight against cancer.

The hospice nurse told him, 'Joe shouldn't still be here. The reason he's not ready to go is because he's worried about you. You have to tell him it's OK for him to go.'

Joey had nearly died twice before from cancer and had lived through three comas caused by motorbike accidents, but his famous brother knew this time really was the end. Mickey got up, shaking, and made the short walk to the bedroom where his little brother had been staying for the past two weeks. He put his arms around him, told Joey how much he loved him and then said, 'If you gotta go somewhere right now, you go ahead and I'll meet you there later on some time. It's OK, because I'll be OK, you understand?'

Joey then took his last breaths – and died in Mickey's arms.

Since his brother's first diagnosis with cancer at 17, Mickey had done all he could to try and halt and then reverse the inexorable march of the condition, including a mercy dash to Mexico for radical new stem cell treatment. He had always come to Joey's rescue when they were kids but he couldn't save him this time and, having battled various forms of the disease down the years, lung cancer eventually claimed Joe Rourke on 6 October 2004. Mickey was shattered.

As Mickey admitted in a 2005 *Sunday Times* article, the one comfort to him was that in the final few weeks of life, Joey said how pleased he was that Mickey had changed for the better and was starting to get his life back on track. He had told him, with relief, 'You've changed, bro', you're not so crazy,' and the older brother cherished those words.

After the funeral, Mickey said a final goodbye to Joey when throwing his ashes into the sea – and noticed a flash of blue light on the horizon when he did so. Since then, whenever he sees a blue light, Mickey believes it is Joey waving to him. He still misses his brother terribly and, in the living room of his New York home, keeps a candlelit shrine to Joey where rosaries and photos of him surround a statute of the Virgin Mary.

The loss of Carré Otis from his life had been Mickey's first significant heartbreak and the next was the passing away of his beloved, bearded biker brother. That tragedy caused him to question his faith in God for the first time. Mickey, who had briefly been an altar boy at the age of 10, stopped going to church for a while and no longer prayed with the same conviction. He couldn't understand why God would take his brother.

Two days after Joey's death, director Tony Scott, who

had worked with Mickey on *Man on Fire*, called to sympathise. His older brother, Frank, had died of cancer and so he knew the agony Mickey was going through. Tony proved a tower of strength at that difficult time and also provided Mickey with some work to go to, offering him a role in his new movie, *Domino*.

It was good for Mickey to be back from the B-movie wilderness working on major movies again because, for most of the past decade, he had been stuck in a career quagmire while suffering much personal misery during what he calls 'my lost years'.

But Joey had left Mickey with something – his spirit. Showing all the determination his late brother had possessed, Mickey resolved to battle his way back to the top.

■　　■　　■

After having to quit boxing on health grounds, Mickey had thought he would be able to make a swift comeback to the acting big time – but it didn't happen. Doors kept slamming in his mashed-up face. He still had the acting talent but, like his early screen idol Montgomery Clift, whose damaged face had to be rebuilt after a car accident, he was trying to relaunch an acting career with a very different look. But film history was full of stars springing back from obscurity, like Mickey Rooney, Marlon Brando, Joan Crawford and many more. Mickey reckoned that in two or three years, he would be next.

Yet mainstream Hollywood didn't want to know. Regardless of his ability or appearance, Mickey Rourke was damaged goods after his wild behaviour of the past and restoring the industry's trust and respect was not going to be easy. The film business had moved on and so Mickey just ended up being cast in low-budget movies that were beneath him but to which his name and renown might add some extra takings during their short cinema run or DVD life. In a few short years, he had gone from starring with Robert De Niro to acting alongside the likes of tattooed basketball bad boy Dennis Rodman.

The major studios with their big pay cheques weren't calling any more and he was having to take very different screen roles such as appearing in a pop video, for the Enrique Iglesias single *Hero*, a BMW commercial and providing one of the voiceovers for a video game, the third instalment of *Driver*.

As years went by and he still wasn't back in major movies, Mickey began to think that all the people who had written him off as a washed-up has-been maybe had a point. Being yesterday's news was hell. It was humiliating for someone as talented and proud as him to be getting little, or little seen, work as an actor. He felt terrible whenever a passer-by would vaguely recognise him in the street and stare, struggling to place the face and the name of the former star. There is a scene in *The Wrestler* when Mickey's character, Randy, becomes similarly upset at a delicatessen counter, causing him to react in frustration by thrusting his hand into a meat slicing machine. It appears art really was imitating life, as Mickey is alleged to have reacted just as dramatically during his wilderness years. He once described to an interviewer, but has not discussed since, how, in a particularly dark mood, he deliberately sliced the top of his little finger almost off, until it was just hanging on by a tendon – and had hours of microsurgery to have it sewn back on.

In a bid to avoid being recognised all the time, he started doing his shopping late at night in a 24-hour West Hollywood supermarket when there were few customers around to gawp at him. Extravagant purchases were a thing of the past as his money had run out. The big house and the big cars were gone, along with his good looks, and his entourage of hangers-on had left him as soon as the money disappeared; some of them even took all they could carry out of the big house.

Court documents show that his LA home was repossessed after he couldn't make the monthly payments – and he owed various people money, not least the tax authorities. He was $60,000 in debt at one point and didn't have the money to pay the therapist who was by now treating him three times a week.

His businesses had gone belly up, including Mickey and Joey's, the small Beverly Hills news-stand and candy store he had owned with his hairdresser pal Guiseppe Franco. Meanwhile, in an effort to stop all his wild spending, Mickey's accountants took his credit cards away from him.

Having given up boxing and with Hollywood not calling, Mickey was living in a $500-a-month one-room apartment, getting by with the money received from the rare acting jobs which came his way, as well as loans from friends and the proceeds from selling his motorbike collection. Every few months, another of the dozen Harleys he had accumulated over the years would go at greatly reduced prices until there was only one left. When he couldn't afford the petrol to put in his car, a 1963 Mini Cooper, he had to sell that, too.

He even wrote his way out of trouble at one point by composing poems and selling them. Mickey made an impressive $16,000 from selling eight framed, poster-sized poems displayed at a special Beverly Hills show. This was a sample stanza: 'I should have been born a statue of stone, I'd have no pain, no place to call home.' It's hardly Wordsworth but it was effective in helping the cash flow.

A poem which would have better summed up Mickey's life at this time when loved ones had left him, the studios no longer employed him and photographers didn't want to take his picture any more was 'They flee from me that sometime did me seek . . .' the best-known work by lyrical 16th-century poet Sir Thomas Wyatt. For Mickey was now Tinseltown's forgotten man and, worse than that, most of the time, the pugilist-turned-poet was completely without the means to pay for everyday items. He had gone from eating in the finest restaurants to regularly dining at McDonald's.

Mickey was in a dark, dark hole. On the rare occasions he got some cash together and felt like forcing himself out to visit a busy and ritzy restaurant on a Saturday night, he found he could no longer get a reservation just by calling up and giving his name. Mickey was sick of going from millionaire movie star to hard-up has-been and wanted to be anonymous. Desperate, he called up an old friend who used to work on his cars and asked if he could fix him up with a job on a building site. The pal laughed as if he was joking and put the phone down.

Mickey would also phone up Carré Otis, crying down the line and asking her to come back to him – but to no avail. He didn't have any big Hollywood dreams at this point – his only dream was that Joey would come back to life and walk in the door.

His respectability and hope gone, gloomy Mickey was widely reported to have often fallen to his knees in prayer, asking God, 'Please can you send me a little bit of daylight?' Things in his life would brighten up for a while and then quickly turn pitch black again.

Having had such a fall from grace, dark thoughts inevitably clouded his mind. He did consider suicide at this time but was stopped from doing so by a combination of his restored Catholic faith, the memory of how bravely Joey had fought for life and a desire not to leave his dogs without someone to care for them.

With the closest relationships in his life, Carré and Joey, lost to him, Mickey felt alone. He had waited and hoped for Carré to come back to him for so long but something changed in him when Joey died and he gave up waiting from that moment. He also stopped talking to his mother completely after Joey died – as his brother had been upset to the end about her turning her back on the sadness they both felt living with their stepfather. Thinking about his anger towards her, Mickey realised that while he loved his mother, he didn't like her – and that he now gave his dogs more consideration.

When he had felt upset as a child, he would go running to his beloved grandmother. That wasn't an option now that she was in her declining years, although she would live to the age of 99, only passing away in 2008. There was no way he was speaking to Gene Addis, he wasn't close to his stepbrothers and his sister had her own life. But Mickey had his dogs – and they were a huge comfort. The unconditional love he received from them kept him going during such dark times. He has adopted a bunch of four-legged friends from shelters, mostly tiny chihuahuas, choosing to rescue dogs who had been abused because their suffering reminded him of how he had struggled at the hands of his stepfather.

The dogs were great companions for Mickey – and became his new entourage. They filled an emotional gap in his life, too, turning his home into a much happier place. Mickey was unable to sleep in his bed for years after Carré left, feeling it was just too big and empty without her, and switched to kipping on the couch instead. But as he took in more and more dogs, they crowded on to the sofa with him and eventually filled up his bed again, too.

Recent scientific studies have shown that the companionship of dogs brings about psychological and health benefits including lower amounts of stress-related hormones and the lifting of depressed feelings. His four-legged therapists really did the trick for Mickey.

His favourite of the bunch had been Beau Jack the Great, who became his constant companion. Mickey was distraught when Beau Jack died in 2002 and tried to bring him back to life, attempting to give the dog mouth-to-mouth resuscitation for 45 minutes until friends pulled him away. When he knew the dog was gone, Mickey took Beau Jack's body to a church to be blessed. He fell into a deep depression afterwards and was only lifted from it by Beau Jack's daughter, a small brown chihuahua-terrier mix called Loki, who took over as his best friend on the planet. She had been the runt of the litter and Mickey had fallen in love with her from the second she was born.

Often seen dressed in a natty sweater, Loki, named after the Nordic god of mischief, was his frequent travel partner and was always at his side in the *Sin City* to *The Wrestler* comeback years.

Mickey was so reliant on the companionship of the dog he called 'the love of my life' that he once spent £3,000 to have Loki flown to England to join him on the set of the movie *Stormbreaker*. He had to have her flown from New York to Paris, then Paris to London, and also pay for someone to come with her – but it was worth it.

He flew with Loki from LA to Austin, Texas, to work on *Sin City*, keeping the dog in a case pushed under his first-class seat – but not far enough under for the liking of a flight attendant who kicked the case while saying, 'Can't you put that somewhere else?' Well, Mickey wasn't having that and roared back, 'Fuck you, you fucking bitch, there's a dog in there. Don't fucking kick it again.' Startled, she did as she was told.

Loki racked up a few film credits herself, appearing on screen with Mickey in *Once Upon a Time in Mexico* and she can be heard snoring in the background of his narration on *Sin City* as she was snoozing on his lap when he recorded the voiceover. Loki also can be seen in her master's movie *Masked and Anonymous*, walking around during Mickey's first scene.

Mickey once told his agent David Unger that if they were on a cruise ship and he and Loki both fell in, it would be the dog he would dive in and rescue – no question about it. The thought of losing Loki was unimaginable.

But, at the grand old age of almost 18, Loki fell asleep and died in Mickey's arms in February 2009, just six days before the Oscars. A couple of days later, downcast Mickey went for lunch at top New York restaurant Nello, where Loki had often enjoyed the carpaccio, and was commiserated over the loss by fellow actor and dog lover James Woods. The loss of Loki looks like being something Mickey will never get over and there are little reminders of her passing every day – like the fact that each morning at breakfast he no longer has to put down a side plate of bacon for her, which she used to love.

When another of Mickey's chihuahuas, Loki's brother Chocolate, died in 2006, Mickey's casting agent friend Bonnie Timmermann paid a special tribute by writing a children's book about the dog called *Chocolate at the Four Seasons*. It was based on the 9½ weeks she spent looking after the dog for Mickey while she was staying at LA's Four Seasons Hotel and casting the movie *Blackhawk Down*. Chocolate would ride to meetings with her in a chauffeur-driven limousine and charmed staff and guests at the hotel, including the chef, who prepared delicious meals for the chihuahua. Chocolate liked his food and enjoyed a gigantic T-bone steak the night before he died.

These days, Mickey's most frequent companion is Jaws, a scrappy white terrier-chihuahua mix, so named because when Mickey first picked him up at an East LA pound and went to kiss the dog, it bit his lip, drawing blood and causing the star to need two stitches. 'I'll take him!' said Mickey.

The other dogs living with him now are Ruby Baby, a white Samoyed who destroyed many pairs of Mickey's designer sunglasses and shoes in her first few months living with him; La Negra, a black pug who rarely sleeps but enjoys watching TV; Bella Loca, another chihuahua-terrier mix with bad legs and other health problems who, when Mickey rescued her from a Texas shelter, had a nail in her head from some debris that flew around in a tornado; and Taco Bell, a big-eared, brown chihuahua. Mickey hasn't always taken responsibility in his life before but he is responsible for his dogs now – and happy to be so.

They all eat well, enjoying meals like grilled pork chops, ground sirloin, boiled chicken breast and spare ribs. The names of all his dogs, past and present, are engraved on a ring Mickey always wears. And when he dies, Mickey plans to have his ashes mixed with those of his dead dogs.

With the help of his dogs, his therapist and his priest, Mickey was gradually able to pull himself out of the doldrums. Yes, he had lost his loved ones and his career was a train wreck, but Mickey wouldn't let this change of fortune beat him. He had never been knocked out in the boxing ring and he wasn't ready to be knocked out by life. Mickey has always been a fighter and now he was against the ropes it was time to fight back. He wanted to earn back people's respect so that when he walked into a room, everyone would look over in admiration rather than pity.

The way to do it was to remind everyone what a great actor he was. All the hard experiences he had had in recent years could surely be draw on to make him an even better, more interesting actor than he had been before. He decided that even if he was in a weak movie, he would give a wonderful performance and get noticed. Mickey had got to the acting summit in the first place by working his way up via small parts and, humbled by his time in the wilderness, he was prepared to do it again in a bid to climb back to stardom.

The former boxer would now learn to fight in a different way in order to secure his future. He resolved not to derail the ambition with self-destructive behaviour, deciding he would stay out of trouble, not shoot his mouth off and behave professionally at all times.

With his spirits renewed and his face rebuilt – it de-puffed courtesy of four lots of reconstructive surgery – Mickey set off on the long climb back to the top.

Helping him get there would be a younger generation of moviemakers – people like Robert Rodriguez and Darren Aronofksy – who had grown up as fans of Mickey and now found themselves in a position to hire him for their movies.

The decline of Mickey Rourke had been one of Hollywood's saddest tales, but the fallen star still had enough hope and determination left to give his story a happy ending.

8

The Wrestler

Mickey Rourke was laid up in a hospital bed at LA's Cedars Sinai Medical Center recovering from an appendix operation, feeling pretty sorry for himself and wondering where on earth his roller-coaster career would go next.

Suddenly, the phone rang in his room and the patient took the call which would change everything. On the other end of the line was Darren Aronofsky, an up-and-coming director about whom Mickey's representatives had often raved. He said he had a project he felt Mickey would be just right for and asked if they could meet to discuss it.

Mickey immediately invited him to come to his room at Cedars so they could talk there but Darren refused saying he had a phobia of hospitals. Aronofsky suggested they instead meet at his office when the actor was better – but Mickey said no because he doesn't like offices.

Well aware of Mickey's eccentric reputation, Darren wasn't at all surprised by that remark and they eventually agreed to meet when they were both in New York a couple of weeks later in a restaurant each of them knew. One of the most rewarding partnerships of both men's careers was about to be launched.

■　■　■

The novelist F. Scott Fitzgerald famously once declared, 'There are no second acts in American lives.' But then, he never saw *The Wrestler*.

That film turned everything around for Mickey Rourke, transforming him from has-been to hot property. It's a story of great drama and emotion – but so, too, is the tale of how the movie was made.

Everything started with the writer, Robert Siegel. He had spent eight years as editor of one of America's most successful comedy publications, satirical newspaper *The Onion*, but eventually got the urge to try a different form of writing. He switched to screenplays but none of the comedy scripts he wrote seemed to work. So Robert instead set out to write something closer to the kind of gritty sports movies he enjoyed, like *Rocky* and *Raging Bull*.

The result was a film called *Paul Aufiero*, which follows the experiences of a car park attendant and self-described 'world's biggest New York Giants fan' who gets beaten up by his favourite player on the team. The screenplay found its way to rising star director Darren Aronofsky, who had made his name with the stylish and edgy films *Pi* and *Requiem for a Dream*, and he seriously considered directing it as his next project.

But Darren passed because his heart was instead set on making a movie set in the world of wrestling – an idea he'd had when he graduated from the American Film Institute and which was inspired by his observation that no one had ever made a serious movie about the sport. Aronofsky had been a fan of wrestling as a kid and one of his fondest childhood memories was of attending a match at New York's Madison Square Garden in the early 1980s.

He needed a writer for the wrestling film he was now ready to make and, as he loved the mood, dark humour and sad drama of Robert's writing, invited Siegel to meet him in a coffee shop where he pitched the idea to him.

The aspiring screenwriter was immediately hooked by the concept and ideas came pouring out of him when Darren got him a copy of the 1999 documentary movie *Beyond the Mat*, which follows several former wrestling stars still performing at local arenas but for little money and despite suffering with various health problems.

The pair agreed to collaborate and attended wrestling shows together where they talked to wrestlers, including veterans such as King Kong Bundy, Nikolai Volkov and Jimmy Superfly Snuka, along the way discovering a deep admiration for such guys and wanting to create a character who would exist as a tribute to them.

Robert, who makes a cameo appearance in *The Wrestler* as a fan getting an autograph from The Ram, worked on various drafts of the script over the next two years while Darren worked on directing *The Fountain*, a big-budget, hugely ambitious, time-travel romance which would flop badly at the box office, and the two would check in every so often and exchange ideas.

Casting was discussed at this stage and both men had only one man in mind for the lead role – Mickey Rourke. Both were big fans of his acting and Darren pointed out that Mickey's own personal mythology had parallels to the character they were creating, who by now was called Randy 'The Ram' Robinson.

When Robert went back to work on the script, he printed out two pictures of Mickey that he taped to his laptop screen as inspiration – one from his handsome, younger days in *Diner* and one looking older and beaten up by life at a recent movie première.

By visualising Mickey in the lead role, his script really started to flow and, after 50 drafts, it was more or less finished.

Siegel, who has since rewritten *Paul Aufiero* under the new title *Big Fan* and made his directorial début with that film, was ready to hand over his script for *The Wrestler*.

He had been paid throughout the writing process by Hollywood studio Warner Bros who were keen to develop the project and release it. But as soon as Warners learned that Mickey Rourke was the man in mind for the lead role, they lost interest in the movie.

Their executives argued, and it was hard to disagree with them, that Mickey Rourke was no longer a box-office name who would guarantee a return on their investment.

But Aronofsky was willing to put his career and reputation on the line to fight for his first choice and felt he would be able to get the movie made somewhere with Mickey attached – even if the budget had to be lower than originally planned. First, though, he had to get Mickey interested in the movie.

Mickey was the first to get to the Greenwich Village restaurant at which they had agreed to meet and, not knowing what Aronofsky looked like, gazed out of the window and quickly worked out which of the arriving customers was the man he had come to see.

Recalling his first impressions of the director, Mickey commented, 'I saw a guy pull up outside on a bicycle in an orange crash helmet. I thought, "What a fucking pussy." He looked real Jewish and real smart and when he walked in he had a swagger about him like his balls were too big for his pants.

'He came over and smiled and still had a smile on his face while he told me I'd messed up my career. Actually he said, "Listen, man, you're a really great actor who's just fucked up your career . . . no one wants to work with you," but he told me he had a project I would be good for.'

Darren outlined the story – about a burned-out wrestler who was once a big star in the sport but is now a has-been living in a trailer park and reduced to dragging his battered body into the ring for small-time bouts – and seemed to capture Mickey's interest. Mickey had no respect for wrestlers and had long thought of the sport as a joke, but he needed a job and so kept quiet.

But then Darren shocked him by telling Mickey he was well aware of the problems Mickey had caused for directors on his earlier films and, if they worked together, he would have to be utterly compliant at all times and respect his authority.

'While pointing his finger at me, he said if I make the movie with you, you have to do everything I say, you never denigrate me in front of the crew. You can't go hanging out all night and I can't pay you.'

The old Mickey Rourke would likely have told him to go fuck himself and his participation in the movie would have ended right there. But after years of therapy and better career guidance, he saw things differently now. No doubt,

Mickey was shocked by the comments but admired the director's honesty. So many moviemakers had lied to him over the years and had later stabbed him in the back that he liked how Aronofsky was honest enough to lay his cards on the table up front.

Mickey took the script home – but hardly fell in love with it straight away. He admits, 'I read the script – and I didn't think it was that great.' His first reaction to Randy 'The Ram' was 'that character is one pathetic son of a bitch'. He also recognised that the character felt shame at his has-been status and didn't know if he wanted to get in touch with similar emotions within himself.

Mickey had trained at the Actors' Studio in the Stanislavski method which encourages actors to personalise everything. So he knew taking the part would mean putting himself in a dark place emotionally by revisiting some painful moments from his own life. But he had faith that he was in good hands with Aronofsky and felt that together they could improve the script and make a very good film. 'I'd heard a lot about Darren Aronofksy for a few years. People who work for me had said he wanted to work with me.'

Mickey would come to consider the moviemaker to be among the very best in the business. 'He reminded me of Coppola. He doesn't compromise. He takes chances. He doesn't make your usual Tom Cruise movie. He's resisted Hollywood's efforts to make him do lousy movies. That sounded interesting to me. I have respect for someone who they throw money at but he says no in order to do his own thing.'

Mickey had some ideas for making the movie better and was happy that Aronofsky welcomed his suggestions and let him rewrite sections of the script. He said, 'One was the scene in the locker room when Ram and the other wrestler are talking about the pharmaceuticals. I had pumped iron with muscleheads at the gym for 15 years and I saw a few things. It was very important not to hide what really goes on. These days the wrestlers are all chiselled up. There are physical requirements your body has to take on, a certain way to look, and people do many things that might harm them down the road.'

As well as adding that scene where The Ram is shopping for steroids, Mickey punched up the dialogue where the wrestler pours his heart out to the daughter he abandoned. He also wrote the big scene at the end where The Ram says he never thought he would be back in the ring again, that he isn't as young or as good-looking as he used to be. That scene was all Mickey, writing based on his own life experiences. But despite all the similarities, Mickey has been keen to point out that he isn't playing himself in *The Wrestler*.

To prepare for the film, he had to come to understand the world of wrestling and learn all the right moves, holds and throws so his fighting skills would look convincing on screen.

His boxing background was no help at all in preparing to play a wrestler. 'The sports are as different as rugby and ping pong,' Mickey explained. While boxing is all about hiding the punch, wrestling is about showing it with exaggerated swings – so he had to unlearn all his established ring technique, including slowing down to the more leisurely pace than he was used to in boxing. Wrestling is all about delaying the result and stretching out the story, whereas in boxing the fighters just want to get it all over as quickly as possible.

'It took me a month and a half to stop fighting like a boxer. They brought in some ex-wrestlers and they worked with me real patiently. I knew nothing about the sport – I didn't even know how to put my tights on.'

But he soon learned wrestling required a discipline and dedication that he had never expected. Those were qualities Mickey needed as well in order to pump up his body for the part. To acquire the physique of a wrestler, he had to gain 35lb of muscle and achieved it by twice-daily workouts with an Israeli ex-cage fighter, including lots of weightlifting, and eating seven meals a day. He was also flinging himself around the ring learning to wrestle, mostly with coaching from the film's fight scenes choreographer Afa Anoa'i who had once been a member of a bad-guy tag team called the Wild Samoans and is the uncle of wrestler-turned-film star Dwayne 'The Rock' Johnson. The actor quickly learned that while much that happens in the sport might be staged, the pain is only too real.

Mickey injured himself so severely in training for the film that he was carted off to the hospital on three occasions – but didn't tell the director for fear of losing the role.

'I'm no spring chicken and I was getting hurt. I told my agent but didn't want to tell Darren. I had three MRIs in the first two months' training for this.'

He blew out a disc in his back, badly injured his knee and also severely twisted his neck.

'I don't like doctors. I was going to an acupuncturist for treatment. After three weeks of hell, I finally went to a real doctor and he gave me anti-inflammatory drugs. I was fine after that.'

But suddenly, during his training for the part, Mickey

Rourke was replaced in the lead role. It had not proved possible to attract financing for the film with Mickey in the part – investors wanted a safer bet, an established movie star. So it was that Nicolas Cage came on board as the new star of *The Wrestler*. Within two weeks of his agreeing to do the movie, the funding fell into place with $15 million readily available.

Mickey's representatives were devastated – but Mickey took the news surprisingly well.

He explained, 'I was really relieved. I knew Darren would want me to revisit some dark places for this role, plus I wasn't being paid, so when they said I wasn't in the movie any more, I was the only one who wasn't upset. Then something happened with the other actor and suddenly I was back on the film and it was back to the training for me.'

He wasn't wildly enthusiastic to be back throwing himself around the ring and visiting those dark, traumatic places. When his agent called to tell him he was re-attached to *The Wrestler*, Mickey even replied, 'Oh fuck, can't you get me something else?'

What apparently happened was that Cage was only available for a limited period and didn't feel he had the time to bulk up his body into a wrestler's physique. He knew Mickey had been attached to the role earlier – and even called Mickey for his blessing before stepping into the part. In working on the script, he saw just how much the screenplay echoed aspects of the life of Mickey Rourke – with whom he had worked on *Rumble Fish* many years earlier but had lost touch with over the years.

After Mickey gave him the go-ahead, Cage started

training but, the way he tells it, soon realised that the only way he could rapidly transform his physique into that of a wrestler was by taking steroids – something he wasn't willing to do. So he resigned from the film, called up Mickey to inform him of the decision and said he hoped Mickey could somehow get the role back.

The fact that he did was all thanks to Mickey's enduring popularity in France, where even flop films like *Heaven's Gate*, *Year of the Dragon* and *Rumble Fish* were hailed as cinematic classics. The only company that would step forward to support the movie with him in it was a French one, Wild Bunch. It proved a wise investment as they would make their money back many times over. *The Wrestler* earned $27 million in American cinemas and many millions more around the world and on DVD.

Wild Bunch provided the film's budget of almost $6 million and that gave the movie the green light – although, given the reduced budget, it would have to be shot faster and with fewer locations than planned. This would be bargain basement moviemaking, a 37-day shoot using 37 locations and with none of the frills of major films. Mickey wouldn't have a luxury trailer or even a chair with his name on it.

But he would be a leading man again. On his first day of filming, the assistant director would shout, 'Bring number one to the set . . .' – and that was music to Mickey's ears as he hadn't been number one in a long time.

Mickey threw himself back into wrestling training and Darren would frequently check on his progress, all the time pushing him to be the best that he could be. Aronofsky felt his leading man had been a little lazy in previous film roles, coasting through the parts without much effort. But he demanded total commitment from Mickey on this film – and got it, too.

Mickey recalls, 'I wanted Darren to be proud of me. He kept yelling at me all the time. I thought, "I'll show you, you prick." So I learned all these wrestling moves and I soon grew to love the sport.'

The star did six months of bodybuilding and three months of wrestling training to get in shape for the part. Many professional wrestlers and fans of the sport who saw the movie would later compliment him for having the look and the moves just right.

Due to the challenges of the reduced budget, the film's wrestling matches were shot at actual wrestling shows with a live crowd, in between the regular wrestling cards they were there to see. The crowds, who love the theatrics of the sport anyway, seemed psyched by the idea of a wrestling movie and all got into the spirit required.

As well as putting himself in harm's way by flinging his fifty-something body around the wrestling ring, Mickey Rourke literally bled for the part. At their first conversation about the movie, Darren had told Mickey about 'gigging' – a trick of the trade which sees wrestlers hide a bit of razor blade in the tape covering their wrists and sneakily pull it out at a key moment in the bout to cut themselves on the face so the blood will flow into their eyes and give the audience a dramatic spectacle. Aronofsky had told the star he would want him to gig in the film – and Mickey had been nervously waiting for that moment for months.

When it came to shoot the scene, Darren told him he really didn't have to do it – but Mickey replied, 'Fuck that,

I'm cutting myself,' and anyone who watches the film can see the results.

Mickey did it as a mark of respect for Aronofksy, who had won his admiration for continuing to be honest with him all along. He explained, 'When he said he wouldn't pay me, at least he said it to my face.'

Mickey did eventually get paid for the film but not that much above 'scale' – the Screen Actors Guild union rate – and a long way short of his big-money paydays of the past. But this one wasn't about the money. 'Darren and I gained each other's trust,' added Mickey. 'I like to work with directors that are smarter than me and are very well prepared.'

But it wasn't all sweetness and light between director and star and the pair had several arguments during filming, about everything from the costumes Mickey would wear to the number of takes he would shoot. Aronofsky was always pushing for more takes, saying, 'I want you to bring it,' and when Mickey said that he just had, the perfectionist director replied, 'Bring it more.' He was like a boxing trainer asking his fighter for one more great round.

Once when he wanted to drain all possible emotion out of Mickey for a scene, he did something guaranteed to push his buttons. Right before calling action, he implied that Mickey's beloved dog, Loki, who had been sick in recent days, had died. It wasn't the nicest thing to do, but it was certainly effective.

There was a certain amount of give and take between director and star but Aronofsky established his authority so that he got the final say each time. When Mickey declared he wanted to wear a hearing aid in the film, he had to fight like hell to get his way. Darren didn't want him using any method actor-style props – in fact, he considers not letting Mickey wear sunglasses his greatest achievement on the film! Mickey justified his choice by telling him about an old wrestler he had met who now wore a hearing aid and Aronofsky relented – but under-used it in the film, so we only see the hearing aid fleetingly.

These creative debates were all about making *The Wrestler* the best movie possible and Mickey was coming to realise that his whole life had been leading up to playing this role. He certainly understood what the character of The Ram was going through as a hard-up has-been. He said, 'Randy The Ram was somebody 20 years ago and so was Mickey Rourke. When you used to be somebody and you aren't any more, you live in what my therapist calls a state of shame. You don't want to go out of the house. I lost everything – my house, my wife, my credibility, my career. I even lost my entourage, which is when you know things are really bad.'

Mickey Rourke was once shopping in a 7-Eleven when a man walked up to him and said, 'Didn't you used to be a movie star?' It was a humiliating moment for the actor and one that is mirrored in *The Wrestler* when The Ram is mortified to be recognised by a wrestling fan when working behind the deli meats section of a New Jersey supermarket. That was the most difficult scene for Mickey to film in the movie as it brought out much of his own shame at how far he had fallen in his own life.

Mickey begged Aronofsky not to shoot the scene or at least give the character a different low-paid job such as a dishwasher, where he would not have to mix with the public. But Darren knew it was a key moment in the movie and felt that Mickey could use his own pain to make it a mesmerising one.

The moviemakers didn't have enough money in the budget to close down the supermarket and fill it with actors, so the store stayed open throughout the filming and real people would often come up to the meat counter and Mickey would serve them while the cameras kept running. As such, a lot of the deli sequences are improvised. Mickey actually got in trouble with the supermarket manager for writing the wrong prices down on the meat containers many of those customers were taking to the register.

Apart from genuine customers, most of the performers in the deli scene were Aronofsky's friends or relatives. The irritating woman who complains about the portion size is Darren's mother. But there were plenty of other interesting casting choices in the film. When Mickey was out with Aronofsky in a club one night, they spotted, standing by the bar, the he-man who would play the steroid-dealing wrestler in the film. Pointing at the hulking stranger, Darren said that that was the sort of guy he wanted in the part. So Mickey encouraged him to go over and offer the man the job.

Scott Siegel was the man in the right place at the right time and he certainly made the most of his opportunity. Mickey calls him 'the one guy who ever stole a scene from me'.

But it's no wonder he seemed so authentic in the part. For it later emerged that Scott Siegel had served four years in prison for trafficking steroids. A few months after the release of *The Wrestler*, he was arrested and charged with the same offence. Officers found 1,500 bottles of anabolic steroids in his home, along with $100,000 in cash. Siegel attempted to flee after cops closed in on him, driving his car through a fence and smashing into five police cars while trying to escape the scene.

Some real wrestlers were used in the film, but they were mid-level draws like Dylan Summers as Necro Butcher and Ernest 'The Cat' Miller, who played Ram's final opponent The Ayatollah, rather than more recognisable superstars of the sport. The director felt that using Hulk Hogan or any of the other better-known wrestlers of the past would hurt the fiction of the story and pull people out of the movie.

Although Mickey didn't really get any staples in his body in the hard-to-watch fight scene with Necro Butcher, Summers certainly did. He was so pumped up for the movie that he fired the staple gun into his forehead five times just in rehearsals.

The Ayatollah was a fictional character but the fact that he was portrayed as evil, wore a skimpy leotard in Iran's national colours and was played by an African-American actor rather than an Iranian one, as a nod to the sham-like nature of the sport, did not go down well with the Iranian Government, who condemned the movie.

When representatives of the US film industry, including actress Annette Bening and Academy President Sid Ganis, visited Tehran in March 2009, they didn't exactly get a warm welcome. President Mahmoud Ahmadinejad's art and cinema adviser Javad Shamaqdari complained about various 'insults and slanders' against Iran in recent Hollywood movies, including *The Wrestler*, in which Mickey Rourke's character smashes a pole carrying Iran's national flag across his knee.

But everyone outside Iran seemed to like the film and, along with great reviews for Mickey, there was plentiful praise as well for his two leading ladies. Evan Rachel Wood, one of Hollywood's fastest-rising young talents, played The Ram's estranged daughter, Stephanie. Because her character and Mickey's were supposed to have been apart for so long, Aronofsky decided that they shouldn't rehearse together or even speak to each other before filming the first scene they shot together. The actors felt his artistic choice worked in the film's favour by making that first encounter between their characters twice as emotional.

By far the most emotional scene of the movie comes when The Ram is pouring his heart out to his daughter, telling her, 'I'm just a broken down piece of meat.' Using all the acting gifts that have served him so well since the Actors' Studio days, Mickey isolated himself for a while to prepare for the scene and when he felt he had reached the right emotional level, walked on the set and performed that scene to perfection . . . but the director wanted him to keep doing it again and again. He recalls: 'I nailed it on the first two takes. Darren wanted to do more. But I'd shot my load, it was all over the room, I was spent, I'd got my shit in the can.

'We did more takes and Evan kept getting better in the scene, I kept getting worse. Then Darren said this word I hate – "Dude . . . " he said, "Dude, she's blowing you away and you suck."

'I said, "As far as I'm concerned, you got what you requested." He said, "You've got to keep giving it to me."

I kept trying to bring it for him and for Evan. It's rare you meet someone like Evan Rachel Wood. She's so focused and natural. She would go off, smoke 20 cigarettes, come back and do a great take. We were working together, you don't get that that often. I've got nothing but utmost respect for her.'

That respect only increased after a scene where Evan ended up bleeding for her art, just as Mickey had done. In their big confrontation scene where Evan throws magazines and a lamp at her screen father, she also picked up a soft drink can to throw at him but cut her finger open on it – and the blood poured out. Darren Aronofsky was concerned about the actress, and also worried about the limited shooting time they had left at the location. He said they could either call an ambulance right then or use superglue to patch up the wound and continue shooting. Evan looked over at Mickey Rourke, who was beaten up from the toll of filming the physically demanding movie, and said, 'I guess we'll superglue my fingers!'

Her character's issues with her father struck close to home for Wood, who didn't have much of a relationship with her real-life father. She would get together with him generally only once a year and those were always frustrating occasions where finding common ground and communication was difficult. But Evan was so moved by the storyline of *The Wrestler* that it caused her to work hard at reconciling with her own dad. She hopes the film inspires others in similar situations to rebuild relationships with their own fathers.

Mickey didn't become a father figure to her – or a boyfriend despite some wild rumours – but more of a cheeky mate. For her 21st birthday, which he helped her celebrate at the Toronto Film Festival, he got her a cake with a pair of handcuffs in it. Evan remembers waking up the next morning handcuffed to a champagne bottle but with no clear recollection of how that happened. But what is clear is that her performance played a big part in *The Wrestler*'s success and Mickey has continued to sing her praises.

Mickey's other female co-star, Marisa Tomei, also won respect from Mickey, from critics and award voters, too, landing the Best Supporting Actress Oscar and BAFTA nominations for her role as Cassidy, the stripper who captures The Ram's heart. Cassidy was written as a mirror image of Randy in that she was also at the end of her shelf-life, getting older and earning her livelihood on stage with a mask of a public persona.

Just as Mickey had to get in shape and learn the right moves for his role as a wrestler, playing a stripper also has its routines and requirements. So, as well as exercising and giving up bread prior to filming, Marisa worked out for weeks with a hula hoop so she could swivel her hips and shimmy perfectly for the part. But she turned down Darren Aronofsky's suggestion that she should perform in a real strip club in front of actual customers as preparation for the role.

Her revealing performance in the film was done in front of hired extras and the crew – but it was shot in a real strip club, Cheeques, in northern New Jersey. In fact, it was so real than Darren Aronofsky – who, incidentally, had attended the same Brooklyn school as Marisa, Edward R Murrow High – had to have the club cleaned before he and his actors could work in it.

Just as he pushed his other actors hard to do better and better takes each time, Aronofsky showed the same determination with Tomei, too. The pivotal dance sequence where she strips, gryrates, flaunts and prances around the pole was actually the 26th take the director had demanded for that scene.

Many moviegoers watching *The Wrestler* wondered how the 44-year-old actress was able to make herself so uninhibited, loose and free in stripping scenes that must have been nerve-wracking to film. The secret could be found in her coffee mug. Marisa asked her personal assistant to keep bringing over her coffee mug between takes – but the actress doesn't drink coffee. She had tequila in there and, after a few swigs, and a few swings around the pole, Tomei was able to let loose.

Along with the actors, another crucial element towards the film's success would be the music. In summer 2008, a few months after finishing his work on *The Wrestler*, Mickey was driving around Miami when his mobile phone rang and the voice on the other end said, 'Hey, it's Bruce.'

Puzzled, Mickey replied, 'Bruce? Bruce who?'

'Bruce Springsteen,' said the rock star who had been a friend of his for more than two decades – after Sean Penn introduced them to each other – but whom Mickey had lost touch with in what he calls his 'lost years'.

Earlier in 2008, Mickey had written Bruce a letter telling him about *The Wrestler*, saying how closely the storyline followed parts of his own life and adding how glad he was that he hadn't ended up like Randy in the movie. He wondered if Bruce would like to write a song for the film's soundtrack. Springsteen had already proved himself the master at cinematic heartbreak with his Oscar-winning song from the film *Philadelphia*, 'Streets of Philadelphia', and Mickey knew he could deliver another elegiac winner.

Bruce recalled, 'Mickey told me a little bit about the character. He said some people invest themselves in their pain and they turn away from love and the things that strengthen and nurture their lives – and he told me this was a guy that hadn't figured that out. So I said, "Well, I know a couple of those guys," and so to the song.' In it, Springsteen sings, '*Have you ever seen a one-legged dog making its way down the street? If you've ever seen a one-legged dog, then you've seen me . . .*'

The Boss was calling back that night to say, 'Listen, I wrote a little something.' The sad but beautiful song, which is called *The Wrestler* and plays over the film's end credits, is the perfect accompaniment to Mickey's heartbreaking performance. Bruce wrote it without having seen a frame of the film, but as Mickey explained, 'He didn't see the movie, but he knows me.' And as a favour to his old friend Mickey, Bruce gave the song to the makers of the low-budget movie for nothing.

After the track won a Golden Globe for Best Song from a Motion Picture, Mickey said, '"The Wrestler" will probably be my favourite song until I go to my grave. Bruce did me a favour and you can't put a price on shit like that.'

It was a gesture repeated by another rock star pal, Axl Rose. The Ram comes out to the ring for his final fight with the Guns 'n' Roses song 'Sweet Child o' Mine' blaring – just as Mickey did in his boxing days. Paying for rights to use the song in the film was way beyond the movie's meagre budget, so again Axl Rose gave permission to use his song for free to help Mickey, and is thanked for doing so in the end credits of *The Wrestler*.

With the movie finished and the music done, *The Wrestler* was ready to be unleashed on audiences, courtesy of a distribution deal with Fox Searchlight, the company which had scored big hits with other small films like *The Full Monty*, *Napoleon Dynamite*, *Little Miss Sunshine* and their latest acquisition, *Slumdog Millionaire*. When Fox Searchlight snapped up *The Wrestler* at the Toronto Film Festival, critics and fans became curious to see what potential they had found in the film and in the comeback to leading-man status of prodigal son Mickey Rourke. But the reaction that mattered most to Mickey was that of the wrestling community.

His opinion towards the sport had totally changed thanks to playing The Ram and he was desperate for the men who had really climbed in a wrestling ring to give the film their approval.

During my post-film Q&A with Mickey, Darren and Marisa, Aronofsky announced that one of those real-life ring legends, Rowdy Roddy Piper, was in the crowd seeing the film for the first time and, stuttering a little, the director nervously asked the big man at the back of the room, 'W-well, w-what did you think of it?'

Roddy replied, 'Yeah, I've got something to say,' then he paused and the three guests looked at each other nervously during the moments of silence. But a moment later he paid the film glowing compliments, got emotional about how real it all seemed and admitted he got 'choked up' watching Mickey's perfect performance.

'When he started crying, I knew we were OK,' smiled Mickey.

At the Los Angeles première of *The Wrestler* a month later, several more real wrestling stars of the 1980s showed up and, to Mickey's relief, they were the ones applauding loudest at the end of the well received screening. The star said, 'Those wrestlers are a great group of guys with a special camaraderie. When they all said they enjoyed it, I couldn't have been paid a higher compliment.'

The American critics raved, too, and Mickey was soon basking in the best reviews of his career with his work in the film called 'heartbreaking', 'deeply affecting', 'among the great iconic screen performances' and even 'skip the Oscar, give Rourke a Nobel prize!'

When the film opened in Britain a few weeks later in early January, it was a similar story.

Sunday Express film critic Henry Fitzherbert declared, 'The Oscar race for Best Actor ends here. Mickey Rourke is taking home the trophy for *The Wrestler* and, if he doesn't, I'll digest my DVD collection.'

Awards buzz did indeed start to grow and doors which had been closed to Mickey for years were suddenly opening for him again. *The Wrestler* opened on 19 December 2008 in just four cinemas in the United States but, powered by full houses and fine reviews, distribution had expanded to 700 by the time the Oscar nominations were announced in late January 2009.

Despite all the acclaim the film has brought him, Mickey Rourke still hasn't seen *The Wrestler*. He doesn't like to watch his films until a few years after making them because he gets irritated by things he wishes he could have changed or takes that were unjustly cut out and says otherwise he would be knocking on a director's door at midnight demanding answers.

But when he does get around to watching this one, he can allow himself to feel proud of a job well done. Mickey admits, 'I gave all of myself in this role. It was the first time in a long time I gave all of myself. It was the first time I felt that since I was an acting student.'

Once filming was completed, he had been keen to go to the wrap party and celebrate. But Mickey was so spent with physical and emotional exhaustion that he couldn't even get out of his chair. As he says now, 'People used to ask me what's the best movie I ever made and I always said I haven't made it yet. But now I say *The Wrestler*. It's the hardest movie I ever made but it's also the best movie I ever made.'

9

And the Winner Is . . .

When Susan Sarandon opened the envelope and announced Mickey Rourke as the winner of the Best Actor award at the 2009 Golden Globes, it was the sweetest moment of Mickey's career.

Everyone sitting at *The Wrestler* table immediately erupted in joy. Darren Aronofsky and Marisa Tomei were beaming and, in her excitement, Evan Rachel Wood spilled her glass of champagne on Bruce Springsteen. On hearing his name called, Mickey's face broke into a smile and he immediately embraced Springsteen. He hugged Leonardo Di Caprio on his way to the stage, tripped on the steps then recovered his footing to collect the trophy from Sarandon and turned to address the crowd.

Everyone in the room had risen to their feet in a rapturous, standing ovation – the only other winners that night to receive such a tribute were Steven Spielberg and the late Heath Ledger. He looked out at the sea of famous faces cheering his triumph, said, 'Wow . . .' and, clutching the most prestigious award he had ever won, Mickey began a memorable speech with the words, 'It's been a very long road back for me.'

■ ■ ■

If things had turned out differently, walking down red carpets and winning awards would be a regular occurrence for Mickey. But, as we know, things went south after his promising start – or, as one director told Mickey's agent, 'The guy was a great actor but he shot off all his own toes.'

The Wrestler provided him with a comeback worthy of Lazarus and made Mickey a fixture at the glitzy and glamorous events that made up the Hollywood awards season of late 2008 and early 2009. With his stringy hair, dark glasses, flamboyant clothes and little dogs, Mickey cut a fascinating figure amid the superstar glamour of these ceremonies.

The march towards awards began at the Venice Film Festival in early September 2008. *The Wrestler* won the prestigious Golden Lion for Best Picture there. That achievement marked the first time all involved in the film started to realise that audiences and critics were really responding to the film and Mickey's central performance which the festival's jury president, director Wim Wenders, called 'truly heartbreaking'.

The buzz continued to grow over the following weeks as more and more influential audiences saw pre-release screenings. It soon became clear that there was suddenly so much audience goodwill towards Mickey Rourke and, as the star showed up at Q&As, special screenings and did the rounds of TV chat shows to discuss the film, it seemed he had a real chance of awards glory.

The only previous awards of any significance that he had won were 1983's National Society of Film Critics Best Supporting Actor award for *Diner* and the 2006 Best

Supporting Actor prize from the Chicago Film Critics Association for *Sin City*.

But now he was being talked about for the first time as a possible Oscar contender – especially after he received a nomination in December 2008 for a Golden Globe as Best Actor for *The Wrestler*.

That month, the prestigious American Cinematheque paid tribute to Mickey's career by screening a series of his best films in Los Angeles. The season started with *The Pope of Greenwich Village* and there was a delightful moment in the Aero Cinema lobby after that screening where longtime Mickey Rourke fans, delighted to see their hero celebrated at last, kept shouting out the memorable Eric Roberts line from that movie: 'They took my thumb, Charlie!'

Mickey appeared in person at the final night of the tribute event, following a screening of *The Wrestler*, and seemed overwhelmed by the adulation from a sell-out crowd. He had received a similar warm ovation weeks earlier at a London Film Festival screening of *The Wrestler*. But there was a reason the world was warming to Mickey. Everywhere Mickey went during awards season, he charmed audiences and interviewers with real humility as he told his comeback story, owning up to his mistakes of the past, saying his career was damaged by his own self-destructive behaviour and expressing his gratitude at being back in the game. He would always make a point of thanking his therapist, his agent and his priest for putting him back on the right path.

With praise poured on him from critics and moviegoers following the late 2008/early 2009 release of *The Wrestler* in cinemas worldwide, he was in good spirits in early January

2009 when arriving at the Beverly Hilton Hotel for the Golden Globe Awards, Hollywood's second most glamorous ceremony after the Oscars. He was one of 300 stars on the red carpet but, as the comeback story of the year, he garnered most of the media attention.

Mickey sat next to Bruce Springsteen on *The Wrestler* table where Darren Aronofsky, Evan Rachel Wood and Marisa Tomei were also gathered, hoping it would be a great night for their film. They were not to be disappointed.

Springsteen won one of the first awards of the night when his title track from *The Wrestler* won the Globe as Best Song from a Motion Picture. In his acceptance speech, The Boss said, 'First and foremost, I'd like to thank Mickey. Without him, I wouldn't have written the song. Thank you for thinking of me, thank you for your inspiration and thank you, brother, for your beautiful performance.'

Mickey was clearly touched and blew a kiss at Springsteen on the stage. He would say later that, at that point, it wouldn't have mattered if he hadn't gone on to win the Best Actor award as seeing his friend Bruce rewarded with a trophy was enough for him.

But the night was only to get better for Mickey a couple of hours later when Susan Sarandon read out the nominees for Best Actor in a drama – Leonardo Di Caprio, Frank Langella, Sean Penn, Brad Pitt and Mickey Rourke – and then called Mickey's name as the winner.

He seemed nervous on stage at first but went on to give the sweetest and most memorable acceptance speech at the ceremony. The winner said, 'I'm not a really good public speaker. I was kind of hoping Robert Downey would come up here and talk for me a little bit. But anyway . . . Several years ago I was almost out of this business and a young man got in touch with me and kind of put his whole career on the line by representing me – and he did one hell of a job. So I want to thank David Unger for having the balls. I want to thank his boss at ICM, Jeff Burke, for not putting him back in the mailroom.

'I worked with a really special director who had to really fight hard for me to be in this movie because he couldn't get no money on my name. Darren Aronofksy. I've said this before, like in sports, especially, which I can relate to, really great players or directors come around every 30 years and I really truly believe that Darren is one of those cats. He brought the best out of me. He's tough . . . and he's smarter than the rest of us, maybe not Steven (Spielberg), but, you know.

'We didn't have a distributor when we went to Venice, then Fox Searchlight came to our rescue, so I want to thank Peter Rice. Also, we had a wonderful cast, the beautiful and talented Evan Rachel Wood and Marisa Tomei.

'Axl Rose . . . we had no money, Axl stepped up to the plate and gave us "Sweet Child o' Mine". I'd like to thank someone who broke his balls a lot, the producer Scott Franklin. I'd like to thank Bruce Springsteen for everything . . . I love you.'

There were a couple of mild profanities in his speech which prompted US broadcaster NBC to activate the seven-second delay switch and fade the screen to black. But it was Mickey's closing remarks which would get the most attention and stick longest in the memory. He finished by saying, 'I'd like to thank all my dogs, the ones who are here and the ones that aren't here any more.

Because sometimes when a man's alone, that's all you got is your dog – and they've meant the world to me. Thanks so much.'

The dog tribute went down well with PETA, People for the Ethical Treatment of Animals, who in the days following the ceremony signed up the Best Actor winner as the face of their latest dog neutering campaign. Mickey was shown in posters posing with one of his chihuahuas, Jaws, under his quote: 'Have the cojones to fix your dog.'

Working with the animal rights campaigners made him more aware than ever before of the vast number of puppies who get abandoned or put down because there aren't enough homes for them and he eagerly spread the message of responsible animal ownership in subsequent interviews.

Mickey got a real thrill later in the month when he was presented with a career achievement award at the Santa Barbara Film Festival by legendary director Francis Ford Coppola. In a graceful acceptance speech, Mickey called *The Godfather* the greatest film ever made and marvelled at the fact he had been able to work with its director twice.

Soon there were plenty of other awards piling up on Mickey's mantelpiece. His work on *The Wrestler* won him a string of honours, including the Best Actor of the Year prizes from the Boston Society of Film Critics, Chicago Film Critics Association, Detroit Film Critics Society, Florida Film Critics Circle, Kansas City Film Critics Circle, Oklahoma Film Critics Circle, San Diego Film Critics Society, San Francisco Film Critics Circle, Toronto Film Critics Association, Utah Film Critics Association and the Washington DC Area Film Critics Association.

He had received nominations for the Screen Actors

Guild Awards and the BAFTAs and now the much coveted Oscar nomination seemed a mere formality – or was it? Winning the Golden Globe, voted for by 85 international journalists, was one thing, but would the thousands of Oscar voters really write his name down? The members of the Academy are a traditionally conservative, largely elderly group and no fans of bad off-screen behaviour. Were they really willing to forgive the sins of the past and reward his comeback performance? Mickey was unsure.

The night before the Oscar nominations were due to be announced at 5.41am on 22 January 2009, Mickey's manager JP Parlavecchio asked him if he wanted to wake him with good news. Mickey replied, 'I don't know.'

The next morning he woke up at 8.30am, realised he hadn't been woken with good news and said, 'Oh fuck.' He had recorded the nominations so immediately watched the playback to see who had been honoured and found that he was among the nominees after all. When he watched Forest Whitaker read out his name as the last of the five con-tenders for Best Actor, Mickey didn't let out a cry of delight but just considered himself 'lucky'.

It was his first nomination – and a sweet moment. In a statement, Mickey said, 'I'm so grateful and appreciative of this incredible honour. I'm tickled pink.' His rivals in the category would be veteran character actor Richard Jenkins for immigration drama *The Visitor* , Frank Langella for his portrayal of disgraced President Richard Nixon in *Frost/Nixon*, old friend Sean Penn for playing America's first elected gay politician in *Milk* and superstar Brad Pitt who aged backwards in the *The Curious Case of Benjamin Button*, the year's most nominated movie with 13 Oscar nods. *The Wrestler*'s only other nomination was Marisa Tomei for Best Supporting Actress. Hotly tipped Darren Aronofsky and Bruce Springsteen were both overlooked.

A few days later at the Screen Actors Guild Awards, Mickey's momentum was halted when he was beaten to the Best Actor prize by Sean Penn – but he still won the majority of headlines the next day due to remarks made to reporters that night on the red carpet. The star of *The Wrestler* revealed he had been in talks about appearing at the WWE's (World Wrestling Entertainment) upcoming showpiece event *WrestleMania* XXV in Houston on 5 April – and hinted he could even fight six-time WWE champion Chris Jericho there. Showing pure wrestling theatrics, Mickey looked into one of TV cameras, pointed a finger and said, 'Chris Jericho, you'd better get in shape . . . I'm coming after you!' He told another interviewer he was going to toss Jericho 'around the ring like a tossed salad'. Soon afterwards, Jericho would say that Mickey had made a big mistake and shown him a lack of respect, setting up the kind of war of words that is common in wrestling. Mickey is sure to have been offered more money to appear at the giant *WrestleMania* pay-per-view event than he got for starring in *The Wrestler*.

Meanwhile, having the star of *The Wrestler* endorse his organisation seemed like a canny move on behalf of WWE boss Vince McMahon to counter some of the negative publicity wrestling has received as a result of Mickey's film – which shows bouts with pre-arranged outcomes, wrestlers using steroids and being crippled in later life. Mickey publicly praised McMahon for transforming wrestling from a sport for fat guys in speedos to one for superfit athletes and said he wanted to do anything he could to support the wrestling community because their embracing of the movie had meant so much to him.

The prospect of Mickey grappling in the wrestling ring for real built into a huge media story and also saw him appear on CNN's *Larry King Live* show. Chris Jericho was also on the programme and vowed to teach Mickey a few things in the ring that he never learned while playing a wrestler in the movie. Mickey took the high ground and avoided a war of words by praising Jericho but left the door open for a possible showdown at *WrestleMania*.

Common sense took over a couple of days later when Mickey's publicist said he wouldn't be going into the wrestling ring for real. Paula Woods told the Associated Press, 'Mickey Rourke will not be participating in *WrestleMania*. He is focusing entirely on his acting career.'

Mickey said at a later Q&A event, 'I have people I should listen to now. So I'm listening to them and trying to keep it all about the acting for now.' Nevertheless, he couldn't resist and when *WrestleMania* rolled around, Mickey Rourke was there in the crowd. He was expected to stay in his seat because as a condition of his participation in the upcoming *Iron Man 2*, that film's insurers had insisted he didn't get in the ring and start wrestling. So he got in the ring and started boxing instead.

As Chris Jericho was finishing a match, he saw Mickey in the crowd and began taunting the actor. Mickey got up from his seat, gave the jewellery he was wearing to the people next to him to hold, slowly walked to the ring, climbed in, took off the hat he was wearing and put it over a ringpost and then advanced towards Jericho in a boxing pose. The wrestler put up his dukes, too, but his fists weren't fast enough for Mickey who caught him with a punch. Then the former boxer threw a left hook which sent Jericho crashing to the canvas – much to the delight of the crowd and the international pay-per-view TV audience. Wrestling icon Ric Flair jumped in the ring, raised Mickey's arm in victory and Mickey took the applause of the crowd before clearing off with a big smile on his face.

But back in February, it was a showdown in the awards ring he was focused on as he battled it out with Sean Penn for the two big remaining prizes of awards season, the BAFTA and the Oscar. Following Penn's win at the SAG Awards, it was now a two-man race between him and Mickey. Penn praised his old friend's performance in *The Wrestler* calling it 'a beautiful piece of work' and saying that he wept while watching it. Penn had won the Oscar once before, for his role as a vengeful father in 2003's *Mystic River*, while Mickey was seeking his first win with his first nomination.

Mickey had put in a string of public appearances during awards season, charming voters with his comeback story, while Penn kept much more of a low profile. The two men met up for a drink at LA's Four Seasons Hotel a month before the Oscars and Penn wanted to look out for his old pal. He advised him to be very careful not to do anything which could be misinterpreted. The spotlight was on Mickey again and it was crucial he didn't give the media any negative headlines. Perhaps he should lay low for a while.

Some felt Mickey's recent visibility might hurt his chances, that he was starting to look desperate. Another turn-off might be that he seemed too much of a renegade to attract votes from older, more conservative, voters. There was also the claim that he was only playing himself in *The Wrestler* – before you can be declared the best actor, people have to believe you are actually acting.

By the time Mickey attended the annual Oscar nominees luncheon at the Beverly Hilton Hotel on 2 February, he was distancing himself from frontrunner status and claimed he didn't expect to win the Academy Award this year. 'I'll probably be sitting out there clapping for Sean Penn,' he told the press.

But after struggling to get a good table in decent restaurants not so long ago, he was grateful to be invited to Hollywood's most exclusive luncheon of the year. Eating humble pie, the changed star said at the event, 'The biggest change since the nomination is the people I burned bridges with are forgiving me for the horrible way I carried myself for many years.'

Rourke, along with all his fellow nominees, received a free Oscars sweatshirt, a book on the history of the Academy Awards and a certificate acknowledging his nomination.

He flew to England a few days later where another big honour was about to come his way. On Sunday 8 February, Mickey Rourke was in London for the BAFTAs, looking resplendent in shiny black suit and wearing sunglasses despite the heavy rain.

As he joined fellow nominees like Brad Pitt, Angelina Jolie, Penelope Cruz and Kate Winslet on the rain-lashed red carpet outside the Royal Opera House, it was like watching luxury cars going through a car wash. Asked by the soaked reporters whether he minded the icy weather that greeted him, Mickey replied, 'It's really cold, but I've been out in the cold for a long time.'

But he was soon feeling the warmth of the love of British voters after winning the Best Actor award, which he dedicated to one of his heroes and friends, the late, great actor Richard Harris. His cheeky and hilarious acceptance speech included a special thanks to Marisa Tomei, of whom he said, 'She's a hell of a talent and it was very brave of her to take her clothes off all the time – I enjoyed looking at her.'

The speech contained two f-words – the first of which came when he thanked Darren Aronofsky for 'giving me a second chance after fucking up my career for 15 years' and the next when praising his publicist Paula Woods for having the hardest job in show business by 'telling me where to go, what to do, when to do it, what to eat, what to wear and what to fuck'. Both f-words were bleeped out by the BBC. Host Jonathan Ross, himself just back on the channel after a suspension for inappropriate behaviour, joked, 'I'm afraid that after that speech, Mickey Rourke is now suspended for three months.' Mickey further lived up to his wild reputation backstage by swigging champagne from a bottle while carrying his BAFTA in the other hand.

The press and the public lapped it up but Oscar voters watching on their TV sets 5,000 miles away may not have been so impressed by the return of the bad-boy image. A leading Hollywood executive who is no stranger to winning Oscars told Mickey that night that the expletive-strewn speech had just cost him the Academy Award by alienating all the conservative voters. In a backstage heart-to-heart, he told him he had done brilliantly by appearing so humble and modest throughout awards season but was now falling at the final hurdle by giving people a glimpse of the uncouth actor of the past.

There had been examples in the recent past of an Oscar frontrunner losing out on an Academy Award following bad behaviour at the BAFTAs. In 2001, Russell Crowe berated the show's producer, Malcolm Gerrie, for cutting his acceptance speech for Best Actor. When it came to the Oscars just weeks later, Crowe's performance in *A Beautiful Mind* lost out to Denzel Washington's in *Training Day*. In 2003, Crowe's film *Master and Commander* was nominated for 10 Oscars but there was no Best Actor nomination for its star. It all goes to show that Oscar voters are notoriously intolerant of bad boys.

But many Hollywood insiders were instead warming to Mickey more and more with each mention of how much he loved his dogs. As the awards and attention piled up for Mickey, so did the presents for his pooches. Friends and colleagues who knew the dogs were the way to his heart bombarded the actor with congratulatory gifts of dog food, treats and accessories. I even sent him a mini black motor-cycle jacket for Loki from Beverly Hills pet boutique Doggie Styles.

But an even more eye-catching outfit was quietly being assembled for the elderly chihuahua. At the Oscars, Loki was due to wear a miniature white tuxedo and black shirt – a replica of the Jean Paul Gaultier one which Mickey was planning to wear at the ceremony. But Loki would never get to show it off on the red carpet. For, after a short illness, the 17-and-a-half-year-old chihuahua whom Mickey loved more than anything in the world died in the star's arms – just six days before the Oscars.

On the day before the Oscars, Mickey used his Best Actor acceptance speech at the Independent Spirit Awards to thank the thousands of strangers who had written him letters expressing their sympathy over Loki's death. He got choked up on stage just mentioning the dog's name. It was a bittersweet moment for still-grieving Mickey 24 hours later when he stepped on to the red carpet for the greatest show in showbiz without Loki beside him. But the dog was there in one way – his picture was displayed on a pendant Mickey wore around his neck. He told the assembled reporters outside Hollywood's Kodak Theater, 'She stayed as long as she could. She left me at a time when she knew I'd be all right. I'd rather have Loki another two years than an Oscar and I told her that.'

Brad Pitt was the next of the Best Actor nominees to arrive and discounted his own chances while telling the press that when he was starting out in the business, Mickey Rourke and Sean Penn were his two idols in acting and so he was honoured to be in the same category as them.

The three-and-a-half-hour ceremony, hosted by Hugh Jackman, got under way with Jackman joking about Mickey's use of colourful language at recent awards shows by telling Mickey he could say anything tonight because the TV broadcasters who normally have a seven-second delay had switched to a twenty-minute delay in case he won.

But it soon started to look like it might not be *The Wrestler*'s night to win anything when, in the first Oscar presented, Mickey's fellow nominee Marisa Tomei was beaten in her Best Supporting Actor category by Penelope Cruz. There was still a long time to go until the announcement of the Best Actor winner and Mickey couldn't sit still in his front row seat all that time. During a commercial break, he got up and sat on the end of the stage talking to Harvey Weinstein until an assistant director ushered him off and back to his place just moments before the ad break was over.

Eventually, once it became clear that *Slumdog Millionaire*, a Fox Searchlight movie like *The Wrestler*, was winning most of the other Oscars it was time for the Best Actor to be announced. The movie world held its breath to see if the gold statue would go to Mickey or Sean and Michael Douglas ended the suspense by announcing Penn as the winner.

Mickey led the applause and was soon blowing a kiss towards his friend when the *Milk* star had the good grace to end his acceptance speech with a tribute to Mickey. The Best Actor winner said, 'I am very proud to live in a country which for all its toughness creates courageous artists who, despite a sensitivity that sometimes has brought enormous challenge, Mickey Rourke rises again – and he is my brother.'

At his backstage press conference minutes later, Penn continued the tribute, adding, 'What I think is sensational about Mickey is that he's simply one of the great poetic talents in acting. He quite literally had me weeping almost throughout *The Wrestler*. I've known Mickey for over 25 years. I can't speak for his consistent sense of me because he's an excellent bridge-burner at times. But we share a close relationship and he is someone I've alternatively looked up to and advised.'

If he was devastated at losing out on the biggest prize after all that success in the build up, Mickey certainly wasn't showing it publicly. He put on a white cowboy hat and happily hit the party circuit later that night, not show-ing any outward signs of being bothered.

He was happily chatting at the *Vanity Fair* Oscar party with GMTV Hollywood correspondent Carla Romano, who recalls him as a most memorable interviewee.

Carla says, 'Although he didn't win that night and had clearly knocked back a few drinks, he seemed seriously pleased to be there and to be part of the action. To be up there made him feel re-invented, re-born and his inner rock star came out in full force, added with a delicious humility.

'But with a touch of the rocker about him and being eccentric and champagne-fuelled does not really make for a safe live interview. As I was talking to Mickey, he became more than a little obsessed with my earrings – they were worth half a million dollars and he wanted them. As the studio crossed to me live they clearly saw Mickey trying to prise those gems off my ears – as a live broadcaster I loved that. He wasn't the usual post-Oscar interview. He was dangerous . . . you knew he was going to swear. But the earring theft came as a huge surprise. I laughed my ass off. I loved it.

'I loved him, too. He's true to himself and doesn't really listen to the publicist, which is rare in this business. I loved the outfit he wore, too. He looked like a cross between Noel Coward and Jon Bon Jovi. He rocked it. Seeing that outfit, you knew it was Mickey even before you saw his face.

'I had never interviewed Mickey before but he was once in my top five sexiest men. I was a big fan in the *9½ Weeks* days. I guess he was exactly what I expected – a little flirty, gentle mixed with rough and answering the questions with a dash of 'fuck' for good measure. He comes across as a bad boy but when you talk to him there is such a beautiful vulnerability in his eyes that makes you want to sit at a bar with him, hear all his stories and give him a huge cuddle.

'Comeback kids are always fascinating but when people rise so quickly and then fall as hard as Mickey did, people want to see the best for them. Mickey has had a hell of a time and plastic surgery made him seem like a freaky weirdo to boot. But now people see a good actor and someone who tried to claw his way back. He is so different to most actors. He is like a broken-down alcoholic genius who has got back on the wagon and is holding on for dear life.

'I would be very surprised if his post box is not jammed full of scripts now. When you are hot in this town you are hot. If he carries on being serious about his craft and getting his life together then Mickey Rourke will continue to rise. If he manages to stay humble, that is. But temptation to believe your own press is huge and can make you a dickhead. I hope he doesn't go that route.'

Academy Award winner or not, dickhead or not, Mickey was back in the ring, a contender again, and a champ in many people's eyes. Mickey Rourke even beat President Obama to the Guy of the Year trophy at the June 2009 Guy's Choice Awards in LA. Announcing the two nominees, Jason Statham said, 'One has lifted our spirits and given us hope . . . Barack has shown some promise, too. One has movie star looks, Mickey can act really well. The winner is Mickey Rourke – the leader of the guy world.'

Mickey gave his unusual trophy, a giant pair of antlers, away to US servicemen in the audience, explaining, 'What the fuck am I going to do with these antlers in my house? I would rather they be on the front of some tank in Afghanistan or Iraq where they're kicking ass.'

It was the last event of a long awards season which had seen Mickey kicking ass and cleaning up – with just one major prize missing. So many fans and friends have told him he deserved the Oscar to add to his award collection but Mickey seems OK with the gap on his mantelpiece. As he told interviewer Barbara Walters in her special which aired on US TV immediately after the Oscars, the award would have been a great honour but it wasn't everything to him. He explained, 'In the big picture, you can't eat it, you can't fuck it and it won't get me into heaven.'

10

Hitting Self-Destruct

Mickey Rourke rocked back and forth on the floor of the closet in his Los Angeles home and thought about ending it all. Carré Otis had left him, his career lay in tatters, his money was mostly all gone and he didn't want to be alive any more. He knew that suicide was a coward's way out and that as a Catholic he shouldn't even consider it but, in his desperation, Mickey just wanted to disappear. His retreat from the usual comforts of normal life was now so profound that Mickey had recently taken to sleeping in the closet, as he found hiding away in there more comfortable than being in his own bed.

As all sorts of dark thoughts clouded his mind, he reflected that he had never felt so alone and so unloved. Perhaps he would swallow a deadly amount of pills or put a gun in his mouth. Then he was joined in the closet by his favourite dog of the time, Beau Jack, who looked up at him sadly and whimpered. It seemed to Mickey that the chihuahua was saying, 'But who's going to take care of me if you go?'

That small noise from a little dog was enough to make

Mickey banish all thoughts of ending his life and pick himself up from the floor. But he was going to need professional help – rather than just the loyalty of a loving dog – to pull him out of the pit of misery in which he found himself. So, after previously thinking shrinks were just for crazy people, Mickey decided to go and see a therapist, a man he simply calls Steve. Now, 14 years later, he is still seeing him.

Therapy has helped Mickey understand that all the rage and frustration bubbling away inside of him comes from the traumas he suffered in childhood. Those sessions with Steve also revealed that he had been living in a 'state of shame', that it was almost like he wanted to be invisible – feelings shared at times by his character in *The Wrestler*.

He has also learned what he needs to do finally to get that emotional boulder off his shoulder and conquer the demons with which he has wrestled since those early days.

With so many troubling issues in his head, therapy was clearly going to be beneficial and Mickey is to be congratulated for seeking the kind of professional help that has made him come to terms with his past and move towards a brighter future.

■　■　■

In the rest of this chapter, leading Los Angeles psychologist Yvonne Thomas gives her expert assessment, showing how a troubled childhood of the kind Mickey experienced can bring on issues of shame, self-sabotage, depression and distrust, all of which can be carried throughout life.

Dr Thomas has three psychology degrees, a private practice and is a media expert who has contributed to books, major TV channels and market-leading magazines, including *Cosmopolitan*. She has not treated Mickey but does work with many Hollywood actors, and suggests ways forward so that Mickey can continue towards making the kind of spectacular comeback personally that he has achieved professionally.

Dr Thomas divides her analysis into five sections – childhood, relationships, bad behaviour, depression and the future. She starts by showing how the sadness of Mickey's early years has impacted his whole life since.

Childhood

Dr Thomas observes, 'The world may see Mickey Rourke as that out-of-control, tough, insensitive, devil-may-care, boxing brute of a man, but learning about him and his childhood shows the potentially real, inner Mickey Rourke. That is a Mickey who is still somewhat a little boy, in pain, scared and confused, one who is deeply longing for love, acceptance, enduring and consistent connections, as well as a visceral need for emotional safety and security.

'In working with patients for almost 22 years, I look at understanding how a person's past connects to the present. Sigmund Freud, known as the "father of psychoanalysis", stated that the most formative time of a person's developing self-esteem and identity is in the earliest years of life. The type of environment Mickey Rourke was raised in directly spawned parts of the man and can explain why he took the path he did.

'As a child, he would literally run away from the emotional pain and angst he experienced upon hearing and seeing his parents emotionally hurt each other and go seek refuge with his grandmother. His lack of a loving, emotionally-connected family helped build a foundation for him that unfortunately was based on the divisiveness and abuse he observed between his parents. Then, when six-year-old Mickey's family split up, he experienced even more loss, confusion and turmoil, especially when he was put in the middle of the tumultuous situation.

'As we know, his mother told Mickey that his dad would be joining the family in Florida after they were to move, while Mickey's dad refuted this and blamed Mickey's mother as the home-wrecker. His dad never did reunite with the family, which allowed Mickey to target his mum as the "bad one" while idealising and glorifying his dad.

'The complete extraction of Mickey's father from his youth probably felt like a gut-wrenching experience to him, replete with huge feelings of rejection and abandonment from his original primary male role model – especially because he was the parent Mickey had felt the closest to and idolised.

'It seems that Mickey innately wants and likes closeness – as evidenced by his longstanding upset when people that mattered to him in his younger years were either not available physically or emotionally to bond and connect with. This was exemplified when his parents divorced and Mickey didn't see his dad for around 20 years. When his mum remarried, he experienced more loss, feeling left out, unimportant and forgotten by the one parent who still remained in his life.

'Young Mickey received many negative messages from the most key people in his childhood about how they seemed to view him and his place in their respective lives.

It would seem to Mickey that his mother saw him as a boy less loveable or likable for her to direct her time, attention or help towards in comparison to her new husband and his five sons upon whom she predominantly focused. Mickey's dad apparently reflected to Mickey that he was so unimportant and valueless to him that he completely eliminated the boy from his life.

'Mickey's stepfather possibly indicated to Mickey that he was so worthless that he could be his emotional and perhaps physical punching bag at times. Adding to all this upset, Mickey felt his mother didn't protect him from this abuse.

'Because of enduring at such formative ages so many experiences involving loss and physical and emotional abandonment, it seems quite clear to me that Mickey came to expect that loss and abandonment were normal for him. Likewise, when he was a bit older, Mickey would find himself zoning out from his new surroundings in Miami and was often a million miles away in his head, presumably as a way to deal with his burgeoning feelings of confusion, anger, resentment and disappointment.

'This seems to have been Mickey's way, though not a healthy one, of coping with his upset. Since his father was no longer in his life and his mother seemed unresponsive, Mickey apparently didn't feel he could depend on anyone for emotional support or comfort and tried to stuff his feelings inside.

'Mickey probably felt a great deal of helplessness throughout much of his younger life – and certainly during parts of his adult life. Even though he made attempts to express his feelings and ask for assistance, his needs and emotions repeatedly were ignored by others. In his attempt to fill his need for personal connection, Mickey was drawn towards and bonded with other lost and discontented peers, unknowingly creating a pseudo family for himself.

'Also, as a teenager and adult, he would dress in avant-garde, feminine garb, perhaps as a way to hold on to his softer side and perhaps as a way to fit in with the misfit peers he had formed connections with, while simultaneously toughening up his external self in reaction to preventing further pain or upset from the outside world.

'Mickey revered his father for his physical strength and physique, continually cherishing the one photograph he had of him – hence the shock Mickey felt when, at his own initiative, he came face-to-face with his dad two decades later and in that one-of-a-kind moment, experienced his father's fall from grace, from muscleman idol to weak older man.

'I believe there was one main pattern of repeated behaviour Mickey adopted from his childhood experiences that explains much of why he has gone through such a lot of heartache and failure, often by his own hand. He has subconsciously replicated experiences involving loss and abandonment. Mickey is, no doubt, entrenched in this type of pattern as he experienced so much trauma related to loss and abandonment during his most formative, vulnerable years.'

Relationships

Mickey Rourke's relationships seemed doomed to failure as he lacked the ability to trust anyone. That was due, Dr Thomas argues, to the two most influential people in his childhood – his parents – abandoning him in different ways; Mickey's father by leaving the family and his mother by not being fully attentive to him while doting on her new husband and stepchildren. Mickey's love life has gone badly wrong with two broken marriages behind him and no steady relationships in years. Is Mickey just not cut out for marriage or close relationships?

Dr Yvonne Thomas offers her verdict, saying, 'Patterns learned in a person's childhood can shape and direct the way the rest of one's life is lived out, for good or bad. Sadly, from his earliest memories, Mickey learned that loved ones can hurt each other with words and actions. He also ostensibly learned that families don't stay together and that sometimes a significant person may disappear from one's life entirely, like Mickey's father did for two decades.

'If a child grows up with a parent who is emotionally distant and is uncomfortable being close physically or verbally, the child may not get many hugs, kisses or loving words from that parent. Unfortunately, this youngster may grow up also feeling awkward with expressions of warmth or affection towards and from others, and may actually interpret the way the parent holds back from him or her to mean that the child is unlovable and unlikable – and not just with that parent, but with people in general.

'The unspoken message the child may take from growing up this way might be if Mum or Dad didn't love him, then no one else could and certainly not someone who isn't tied to the child by blood as a relative is.

'In Mickey Rourke's situation, the earliest messages he apparently received about his world were those of turmoil, unhappiness and lack of physical and emotional safety, given the overt volatility and tenuousness of his parents' relationship with each other. It was a pattern he was to play out later in his own most significant romantic relationships.

'With his first major love, his wife Debra Feuer, he could not sustain the closeness very long, even though things were going well for him in his career and in his marriage.

'Instead, Mickey spent increasingly more time engaging in activities apart from his wife, many of which were destructive both to him and to his marriage, including hanging out with his male friends, drinking, possibly abusing drugs, spending a lot of money on luxurious purchases, and ultimately going out with other women.

'Furthermore, he displayed jealous, over-controlling behaviour with Debra, phobias and insecurities that further alienated the couple and eventually culminated in their divorce.

'It seems that Mickey did almost everything humanly possible to sabotage the relationship he had, probably because being in something loving and free of turmoil and unpredictability was an unknown entity to Mickey and, ironically, probably felt even more scary and uncomfortable than the tumult he eventually injected into the relationship. Mickey had not really experienced being in any relationship that was happy and healthy very long. Thus, I doubt that he had any idea what he was doing or why he systematically was sabotaging his marriage.

'Again, Mickey sustained loss and abandonment when Debra left him and he seemed to have suffered tremendously with her departure. Similarly, in his next meaningful love relationship with another actress, Terry Farrell, things couldn't stay peaceful and stable for very long either. There was plenty of passion, apparently, but not just of the positive nature.

'Apparently, Mickey and Terry went through many break-ups and emotional highs and lows together, partly due to Mickey having to hide his relationship with Terry from his adoring female fans who thought he was single. It seems Mickey may have been tempted by pills and attention from other women in this period. So this two-year relationship was terminated as well, chalking up another mark in the "loss" column for Mickey.

'After this, Mickey got involved with Carré Otis, in a very intense relationship. Carré would later become his second wife and was a woman with whom he would experience even more anguish and pain due to the disastrous combination of their respective demons and addictions. The ups and downs of their relationship were proportionally matched with amazing highs and horrible lows. Mickey and Carré allegedly went through physical violence and drug abuse and the relationship ultimately ended up with Mickey reportedly going into a psychiatric hospital after Carré left him.

'This loss may have been the hardest one for Mickey to comprehend or accept because he waited ten years for her to change her mind and reconcile with him, which never did happen. Alas, but true to form, Mickey sustained another episode of significant loss and abandonment to add to his pile.

'Presently, Mickey also remains estranged from the first most significant woman in his life, his mother, partly because she asked him to buy her a house when he became financially successful and largely because she didn't safeguard or emotionally care for him when, as a child, he reached out to her. In addition, Mickey's father died of alcoholism not long after Mickey, as an adult, had reunited with his dad for the first time in almost 20 years.

'In summary, it is no wonder, with the accumulation of all of these gruelling and painful experiences of loss and abandonment, that Mickey would become so distrusting and reluctant to having close relationships with new people who could also potentially hurt him in one way or another.'

Bad Behaviour

Why has Mickey behaved quite so badly down the years, inflicting harm to his career in the process? Dr Thomas says, 'Mickey has a long history of torpedoing his life by engaging in behaviour that has been damaging and destructive – often to those causes that have mattered to him the most.

'He created an irreparable chasm between his first wife, Debra Feuer, and himself by acting out in a multitude of egregious ways, and was arrested for domestic battery against his second wife, Carré Otis. While no charges were brought there he did engage in other misdeeds against Carré, and often defied authority and the law, sabotaging his own progress with his schooling, baseball, boxing, part-time jobs, off-Broadway shows and Hollywood bigwigs.

'Through his pro boxing contests, Mickey also sustained some irreversible damage to his box-office-appealing face.

'Largely because of his background, Mickey unwittingly has been undoing the good things in his life over and over again. Various factors have caused and contributed to the star's self-destructive actions and roller-coaster experiences. It seems that he was mostly taught, directly and indirectly, to be distrusting that people or situations could remain constant and to not value or care much about himself. As a whole, Mickey seems to have learned to view himself with disdain and negativity and carry so much shame with him that unfortunately caused him to subconsciously continue to play out these feelings in new situations throughout his life.

'Certainly, Mickey did receive some positive messages about himself and loving interactions growing up, such as with his maternal grandmother and with some school chums but, overall, the influences were negative and that had an impact.

'Whatever defence mechanisms someone may use to shield themselves from reality, the monsters don't really ever go away. They are there, even if forgotten and out of sight, causing havoc in some form or another, directly or indirectly in one's life.

'I offer suggestions for sustainable, healthy changes later in this chapter. My hope from all of this is that insight can be gleaned and empowerment genuinely felt by Mickey and any others who sabotage their lives in whatever ways they do.'

Depression

How did Mickey become such an isolated and sad figure? Dr Thomas's response is clear. 'It seems that the authentic Mickey Rourke has always been a sensitive person, one who actually feels more deeply than others may readily realise and one who craves to take care of others, especially those in need like his physically ill brother, troubled women or abused dogs. He also has demonstrated his loving, warm side that can connect with and care for those beings that pose no threat to him – such as those dogs and his brother, Joey.

'But as we have seen from Mickey Rourke's life story, a person of such intelligence, heart and talent can spiral down to rock bottom in his love relationships, career and life and even seriously entertain the idea more than once that suicide might be the best solution to his troubles.

'Mickey has experienced so many versions of loss and abandonment over the years – such as death, divorce, emotional and physical rejection and unavailability and failure. Those experiences became familiar to him and caused a lot of pain. As time went on and Mickey had been hurt enough times in his life by people that had greatly mattered to him, starting with his mother and father, he isolated himself from any further deep human closeness. When people got too scary, erratic or disappointing to depend on, he instead allowed dogs in to fill his enduring, core need for companionship, closeness and emotional security, but on a more safe, unconditional love-type of basis, which dogs can often provide better than humans.

'Mickey had regressed back to a childlike state when he was in his closet and contemplating suicide but was convinced he shouldn't go through with it by his dog's cries not to be abandoned. It was like his own abandonment fears while growing up.

'Happily, Mickey abandoned the idea of doing away with himself and sought therapy.

'In spite of all the trauma he has suffered, it actually is a healthy sign that there is still a part of Mickey that yearns for closeness and comfort and which he has allowed himself to find through connecting with and caring for his dogs. I believe these relationships have been very healing for Mickey, providing him the safety, security and consistency he so rarely has experienced with people.

'It would be even better if Mickey could also experience how human relationships could provide some of these comforts and I will suggest how that might happen in the future.'

The Future

So, will Mickey Rourke conquer his demons and find a happy and settled future – or is he going to screw everything up again? Dr Yvonne Thomas remains positive. 'There is hope for Mickey as he continues his therapy. Greater self-awareness and self-knowledge can hopefully help provide enough courage and commitment towards healing wounds and ultimately finding true inner peace, happiness and love.

'For durable, sustainable, healthy changes to occur in a person, it is critical to identify and understand the various factors that have led to their unhappiness and failures so that patterns can be targeted and broken, self-esteem saboteurs can be pinpointed and eradicated, and a person can feel deserving of and working towards self-love and love from others.

'Firstly, for anyone to attain real success in becoming an emotionally healthier person, one must be able to admit that you have issues that need to change. The good news is it appears that Mickey has accepted responsibility more than once about being the cause of many of his own problems.

'The next step is to be willing to actively do something about one's issues, whether that involves seeking therapy or finding another way to resolve one's dysfunctional thoughts, behaviour and/or feelings. Again, Mickey has definitely taken this step, initially fighting his fears about going to therapy and in the 14 years of sessions since then, apparently learning to face himself and his issues – which usually is the part of therapy of which a person is unknowingly most afraid.

'In furthering emotional growth it is imperative to look for ways to refute one's own negative, inaccurate thoughts, beliefs, feelings and actions that limit, diminish or harm oneself and one's life experiences. One powerful way to do this is by venturing out into the world in small steps and trying out low-risk ways to test the waters. This is what psychologists call "reality testing".

'For Mickey, his first step with reality testing might involve him connecting with other animal-lovers or dog owners, be it at a dog park or dog-training class, since there is already that built-in safe commonality of everyone owning and caring for their dogs. Experiencing non-threatening social interactions with people that can actually involve positive, bonding experiences and continuing to build from there with other experiences hopefully can provide Mickey the safety, security and evidence that some people can be loving, consistent and, maybe, even worthy eventually of letting into his life at a pace he can tolerate.

'Certainly for Mickey to heal effectively and move forward in rebuilding a healthy self-esteem and self-image, he must be able fully and freely to grieve the losses and abandonments he has sustained in his life, whether self-created or through life's circumstances.

'Through the safety of his therapy and, hopefully, with some support systems including the comfort of his loving dogs and eventually some trusted humans, Mickey can release in productive, healthy ways the bulk of his pain, hurt, disappointment, anger and confusion connected to the upsetting events he has experienced.

'By doing this step, Mickey then can have more emotional space to heal the wounded little boy who still lives within him. From there, maybe for the first time ever, Mickey can learn how to see himself finally as someone who is truly worthy of love both from himself and from others, as well as how to be in a mutually supportive, nurturing relationship with others, at last being free from the shame, self-sabotage, depression and mistrust that has controlled Mickey's life for far too long.

'Despite experiencing a succession of losses and abandonment throughout his life, this is a man who has continued to show he still wants love and certainly has exhibited the ability to give love back.

'I commend you, Mickey, on having the courage and commitment to continue on your journey to find inner peace, happiness and love. You will find your goal is definitely worth it. As much as you have impressed people with your acting achievements and professional resurgence, your efforts to heal and love yourself are the greatest inspiration of all.'

11

Soul Mates

Macho Mickey, who so often plays fearless tough guys on screen, cried his eyes out on the day he got his left ear pierced. In fact, he was flinching with fear before the needle even touched him.

A witness to the comical moment was make-up artist and hair stylist Teddy Antolin, who befriended Mickey during the nine years he prepared him for various photo shoots.

Teddy recalls, 'We were in the middle of a photo shoot in 1986 when Mickey suddenly wanted to get his ear pierced. This big lesbian, who looked like a man, showed up to do it and Mickey said he only wanted his left ear pierced because the right is gay, or something.

'Anyway, she didn't even get the needle close before Mickey started flinching. The piercing started, Mickey started to cry and his ear got all pink. I told him, "Mickey, keep still, the needle's not that long, it's not going to go in your heart." But he was like "Aaaarrgh!"

'She finally did it but we couldn't resume the shoot until it stopped bleeding. After a while, I was like "It's not bleeding". But it wasn't until an hour or so after she left he was finally emotionally ready to be shot again.'

■   ■   ■

Teddy, now one of LA's leading hair professionals, is one of many old friends with fond and amusing but occasionally disturbing memories of Mickey. He recalls Mickey having very definite ideas about his appearance. 'Mickey was always very opinionated about that. He told me he had been to hairdressing school. He also got knowledge from his wife of the time, Debra, and from all over the place. He would sometimes bring his own scarves and shoes to use in the pictures.

'Mickey certainly knew how to work that hair of his. He would always comb his own hair and then I'd fine-tune it. He wanted it to look like it wasn't combed, like he'd done it with his fingers, even though it had taken 15 minutes to get to that point.

'The only advice I gave him with make-up was "Keep it light" – but he never wanted to. He always liked to wear a lot of make-up in photos. He took contouring to an extreme level and really liked doing eyebrows, jawlines, cheek-bones and giving himself a little colour in his cheeks.

'I know he didn't watch his own films but he always looked at the polaroids taken during his photo shoots, to see how things were progressing.

'Mickey was really sexy back then with a great smile. He is a star because he has that "X" factor, that deliciousness. But he was insecure. I don't think he really liked the way he looked. Mickey had a little bit of acne, he had some acne scars. I detected a lot of insecurity in him. He never projected it but it was just there. I can just tell. Nobody else picked up on it but me.

'I think he wanted to look more Italian – anything but Irish! He wanted to look smouldering. I think that's why he loved the make-up so much and then he went into the plastic surgery. I know why he did that – he wanted cheekbones, he wanted a jawline.

'The first thing he did was the cheek implants. I was on the road with David Bowie in 1990 and his record company threw a big party for David in a Los Angeles restaurant called 72 Market Street. Terry Farrell, Mickey's ex-girl-friend, came with me to the party and it was lots of fun.

'I went up to Mickey there and I pinched his cheek, which I always did to say hello. I didn't know he'd had them done until I walked away and Terry said, "You pinched his implant – he's just had implants!" That was the beginning of it; from then on I would see him around Hollywood and the look got worse and worse.'

It's interesting at this point to note that Mickey's ex-wife Debra Feuer publicly claimed that Mickey got cheek implants around this period but said when she challenged him about it at the time that he told her his face was swollen because he'd had his molar teeth removed. He said the same when there was press speculation about why his face looked different in the film *Wild Orchid*.

Teddy Antolin also remembers Mickey's behaviour around this time. He says, 'Also, Mickey wasn't being so likeable towards the end of the period I worked with him, which was around 1982 to 1991. I think he turned into a bad boy. That happens in Hollywood. After doing the movies he did he was like a rebel. He wasn't like Patrick Swayze and those clean-cut guys of the 1980s. I think he started to take on the rebel personality of the characters he played in the movies. Actors start believing their own PR. It happens. He became a characterisation of himself.

'It first started to get strange when we did a photo shoot with Japanese *Cosmopolitan*. Mickey wanted to art direct it himself and started putting his big fingers into the make-up and smearing it on the model who was in the shoot with him. As the Japanese people from the magazine watched, Mickey turned it into the darkest photo session ever. It was like a precursor to that movie he did, *Angel Heart*. He was pouring water on the model's head, pulling her hair back, ripping her blouse – all the Japanese stood up and turned their chairs to face the wall. It was, like, freakish.

'I left thinking, "What did we just witness?" It was so weird. I thought, "What's wrong with you, Mickey? You were so cute and so sweet." He'd been such a nice guy, we would hang out and he even gave me three designer suits and a hat as presents.

'Mickey got really gross towards the mid-1990s. I'd run into him in places and he'd really say the foulest things. He really wasn't working then at all. He didn't look disfigured yet, just different. He was just nasty to people.

'I saw him in this restaurant on La Cienega Boulevard in LA . . . everyone was outside on the patio, he was sitting by the door with Carré Otis and he was just berating her in public and humiliating her and everyone was like "Jeez, why doesn't he just shut up?" It went on and on. I didn't want to leave until they left in case he took a swing at me. We couldn't wait any longer so we left really quickly but he saw me and said, "What about you, you cunt . . . aren't you going to say hello to me, you little cunt?" and I went, "Mickey, just cool it." It was like he just wanted to fight.

'When he switched careers to become a professional boxer, I'm sure boxing was therapeutic for him. I just hope for Mickey that he doesn't go back to his arrogant ways. I'm happy that his acting career is going well again now but I didn't think he'd come back like this and win all those awards. *The Wrestler* is like his story but in the character of a wrestler. It's him. In the film, with all that long blond hair, he looks like a cross between Hulk Hogan's wife and the cowardly lion from *The Wizard of Oz*.

'As for his look off screen, he's now sort of grown into that face. It doesn't look as bad as it did eight years ago. If what happened to him happened to anyone else, they'd only be playing the Phantom of the Opera.

'He's an intriguing person to look at. But he now looks a little messy to me. I think he has extensions and he's probably still putting hair product in it. That look is great when it's your own hair. Mickey would look better if his hair was just slicked back, like Valentino. You don't want to see all that hair hanging. You're going to see that face with hair or no hair. But surrounding it with a moustache is a mistake, I'd get rid of that. It looks Asian, or like the boxer Manny Pacquiao. With make-up to make his face look moist, I'd make him as dreamy as possible.

'I think he's dressing wrong, too. There's too many little bits and pieces, like the shiny jewellery and that horrible chain around his waist. He needs to be a little bit cleaner. That look works on an 18-year-old skateboarder but for him there's too much going on. I wonder how Mickey feels now when he sees old pictures of himself like he used to look . . .'

Joe Wheeler, who still works as the doorman of Mickey's old apartment building, chuckles, 'I'll never forget the time Mickey set his apartment on fire!' Mickey lived in Unit 11 on the ground floor of Granville Towers in LA from 1999 until 2003. Joe recalls, 'One time, Mickey put a TV dinner in the oven to cook, went in the living room and fell asleep.

'I was working that night, looked over and saw all this smoke in the hallway. So another doorman and I rushed over, saw all the smoke was coming from Mickey's place, knocked loudly on his door, got him woken up and took care of it.'

Joe adds: 'Things were always happening to Mickey. One day we had to bandage him up after he got stabbed outside. He'd just gone out for a coffee and some guy attacked him on the street. The guy actually stabbed him and sliced Mickey's arm. Mickey got the guy off of him but came home and was bleeding. We have a first aid kit in the lobby and dealt with it. After that incident, we'd joke whenever he went outside, "Do you need company today?"

'He felt comfortable and secure in his residence but I don't think he felt as comfortable out there in the world, it was just a feeling I got from him. He had a lot of trouble as far as the streets go because people looked at Mickey as the bad boy. People remembered his boxing career and thought they could take him. They would push him and try to goad him into a fight, like that guy with the knife.

'But Mickey was a quiet gentleman who stayed to himself mostly. The people that knew him liked him. Others that didn't were either scared of him or wanted to challenge him to something.

'My experience with him was nothing but pleasurable. He was never rude or nasty to me and I never heard any complaints about him. None of the other doormen had anything bad to say about the man.

'He was down-to-earth. Granted, he had limousines picking him up here and taking him different places, but he wasn't ever like "Hey, I'm Mickey Rourke!" Once he got to know you, Mickey was very magnificent. In fact, he once tried to get me a job working as his driver. It didn't come together but I was grateful to him.

'He was one of many big names we've had at the Granville. This building goes back to the 1930s and has always been associated with Hollywood people. Everyone from Greta Garbo to Paris Hilton has paid a visit at one time or another. Brendan Fraser from *The Mummy* movies lived in that same two-bedroom apartment as Mickey. He moved out of it and Mickey moved in – with his dogs.

'I remember he loved those dogs. He only had three with him when he was here. Beau Jack, Loki and another chihuahua. We have a dog run out the back and he would take them there. They never pooped in the lobby, Mickey wouldn't tolerate that – he wouldn't even tolerate poop in his own apartment. His home was very neat.

'But his clothes were very exotic. He dressed exactly the same ten years ago as he does now. You would never see him walking around in a t-shirt and shorts. It would always be an exotic combination of clothing. That was Mickey's style. He always dressed differently to other people whether he was going out for a coffee or going out for the evening.

'I saw a few of his friends here but mainly he would go

out to them. He never brought too much home with him. He was single when he lived here but I think he was still very in love with his ex-wife Carré Otis, that's my personal opinion. I got that sense because of the things he talked about. When he brought her up there was a different tone in his voice. I took it as a respect and a love still held. He'd go out with somebody but he never had any other relationship here. He never brought the same girl back here twice unless it was a friend.

'I'd always thought Mickey had great acting ability and was aware of his earlier film work but I hadn't seen him do anything else in years. At times during those years at the Granville I got a sense he was down. I think it wore on him that he was just doing nothing. I don't think he liked doing nothing. Mickey seemed to like being an active person. But you can only be active if there's something to do.

'I am so ecstatically happy that Mickey Rourke is back working a lot now and is having all this success. I hope he makes millions and millions, I truly do. Given the right roles, I think he'll blossom into an actor just as good as De Niro or anyone else.

'I don't care what the world thinks about him, I think he's a great man. It's been my pleasure to know him. I'm thrilled he's back and wish him all the best.'

When Mickey's friend Joe Rivera, one of America's leading fitness trainers, went to see *The Wrestler*, it was like a window into his pal's soul. He explains, 'The heartbreak in the scene of him dancing in the bar with Marisa Tomei, well, that's Mickey. He's trying to be happy and all right but stuff is breaking up on the inside and that inner turmoil is surfacing a little. That's kind of what he's like in real life.

Mickey's a sweetheart of a guy but also a tough cookie and a troubled soul. He really brought himself to that part.

'To be a good actor, you have to be in tune with your feelings, like he is, in order to find the truth of a scene. I know Mickey had a troubled past and had come from a rough background. I'd told him I was from East Harlem, which was tough, and he told me that Miami, where he was raised, wasn't that great either. It wasn't always like it is there now. You could tell from listening to him talk about it that he'd had a tough upbringing there. You knew this was a guy who'd experienced real danger, pain and heartbreak.

'He did a really amazing job in *The Wrestler*, physically, emotionally and performance-wise. I started out as an actor and one of my teachers back in New York would always say the best actor never gets caught acting and therefore the best actor ever was Lassie, because he was so real. In this movie, Mickey was Lassie.

'When I moved out to LA from New York, I never expected I was going to be rubbing elbows with people I grew up watching on screen and when you get to know them you never expect they are going to be regular cool people – but that was my experience with Mickey Rourke.

'I first met him in 1998 at Gold's Gym in Venice, LA, where he worked out next to me. That was great for me as I really respected him as an actor and especially admired the work he had done in *Body Heat*, *The Pope of Greenwich Village* and *Year of the Dragon*. He was someone I aspired to be like.'

As it turned out, musclebound Joe would become a superstar in the fitness world rather than in films and is now known as 'the trainer to the trainer to the stars' – to show his elite status. He says, 'It's funny where life takes you and it's funny that I would keep bumping into Mickey time and again over the years and we became friendly. Because I taught boxing and had fought some amateur fights, he connected with me over that and loved talking about boxing. Every time I ran into him he'd say, "Hey, Joe, you still boxing? I used to box but I can't any more because the doctors told me if I get hit in the head, bad things are going to happen." He would say the same thing every time. It was sweet.

'We used to run into each other at the same cool restaurants and clubs – and at one of those I realised Mickey was a true friend. At the end of the 1990s I was dating this model and her room-mate was the most famous fitness model on the planet, a really nice-looking girl but she wouldn't give me the time of day. I remember her trying to get into Atlantic, the hot place in LA at the time, when I was there with Mickey and she was outside in the line.

'The crowd at that place were like characters from that movie *Swingers*, a cool bunch of hipsters who, even if they came from Bumblefuck, Missouri, they'd adapted their personalities and would give you that New York vibe. If you were some fitness model from rural Texas dressed in a skimpy, tacky outfit, you'd look so out of place there that you were never getting in – no matter how good-looking you were.

'But that night she suddenly saw me pop from behind the velvet rope, shouted, "Joe!" and started chatting me up. Suddenly, she was my best friend. She asked me to get her in, so I had a word with the bouncer and he let us in. Once she was inside, she went right back to not giving me the time of day . . . until she saw me standing at the bar drinking with Mickey Rourke!

'When I stepped away to go to the bathroom, she went straight over and tried to start up a conversation with Mickey, not knowing that I'd just been telling him what a user she was. So she says to him, "You know Joe?" He says, "Yeah, I know Joe," and she goes, "I know Joe, too!" So I get back and Mickey quietly tells me the girl is dropping my name to up her status and have conversations with the people in our group.

'Then we order a round of drinks and Mickey, in the style of his "drinks for all my friends" character in *Barfly*, points out the fitness model to everyone, raises his glass and toasts, "To Joe's new best friend!"

'Surprisingly enough, she got the message and left immediately. But Mickey showed me in that moment what a good friend he was. Being a movie star, he could easily have slept with her – but instead he chose to hang out with friends. I thought it was so cool that he stuck up for me. Most guys in his situation wouldn't have done that. They'd have been like "Who's Joe? Forget Joe . . . Joe Schmo. Hot girl, smoking body, half-naked already – let's go!"

'When you party with Mickey Rourke, it's fun and festive and there's no tension. He's warm-hearted, matter-of-fact, down-to-earth and kind of cool. But he can party hard. I gotta tell you, the boy can drink. He can definitely drink. If you're partying with Mickey, don't try to keep up with him, he'll hurt you. He likes his tequila but he can hold his liquor. I've seen him pounding shots but I've never seen him drunk or falling on his face like the rest of the people around us. There would always be lots of booze, a flock of people around him, hot girls everywhere. Things don't change. I was at the House of Blues in LA earlier this year and was told I'd just missed Mickey Rourke who had supposedly shown up with a bunch of Playboy Playmates.

'It's great that he's been welcomed back by Hollywood and I hope he keeps going on the path he's following now. If he'd won the Oscar this time it would have been the perfect *Cinderella* story but there's no reason why he can't be in that position again. He's always had the talent.

'Things weren't going so well for him a few years ago. He was apparently living beyond his means in that period. People who went to his home would say when you opened the refrigerator there was nothing in there – and it looked like he was going through a rough patch. But you didn't get that sense from Mickey himself. I've never noticed him being depressed. He's not the loud guy in the crew, he's more introspective and doesn't really talk about himself much.

'I gathered things weren't so good around six years ago when I was coming back to LA from a bachelor party in Las Vegas. My flight got delayed and I saw Mickey sitting on the floor with the hordes of other people who had been delayed on a Southwest Airlines flight. That's not the airline you fly when you have lots of money and there he was sitting with the masses waiting two hours to get on the plane. He looks over, smiles and says, "Hey, Joe! Are you still boxing? Because I used to box but I can't do it any more . . . " So sweet!'

12

Chic Unique

When Mickey Rourke rocked up at Moscow's bleak Butyrka prison wearing blue designer moccasins with red tassles, it was clear that a true fashion individual had arrived at the grim building.

The fancy footwear he chose that day in the stark surroundings where he was researching his Russian villain role in *Iron Man 2* was typical of his flair for out-of-place outfits. From the jails of Russia to the red carpets of Hollywood, Mickey can always be relied upon to wear something weird but somehow wonderful. For fashion is a passion and he has developed a style which is uniquely Mickey. Many may laugh at his madcap ensembles but Mickey is his own man and loves his flamboyant look.

And Mickey's awareness of controlling his image extends far beyond his choice of attire. Mickey now tucks his left hand into the waistband of his trousers whenever he's having his picture taken on a red carpet. It's a move which has become as much of a signature pose for him as Victoria Beckham's 'Posh' pout or Paris Hilton standing with one hand on her hip.

When he started doing it at the January 2009 awards shows, it just looked weird and maybe more suited to a rock star, but since then the confident, casual gesture has become an accepted part of the whole eccentric Mickey Rourke look. After all these years of being photographed, he knows his best angle and the hand down the pants is the familiar pose he strikes when ready to show off his latest fashion ensemble to the best effect.

■　　■　　■

This strutting peacock of a star certainly makes the most of a variety of fashion trademarks, including the ever-present chain, big open-neck shirts, unbuttoned cuffs, feminine scarves, shiny suits, tinted shades and fancy shoes.

While most men have only a few pairs of shoes, and then usually only in black or brown, Mickey is the male version of Imelda Marcos and has countless colourful pairs, including some especially striking ones in metallic orange, shiny gold-and-silver trainers and a pair of burgundy velvet slippers. His favourite shoe designers are Jean-Michel Cazabat and Roberto Cavalli.

When one of his hugely overweight suitcases was examined at London's Heathrow Airport in February 2009, it was found to be full of nothing but shoes. Officials first thought he must have put his heavy BAFTA Award in there, as he was on his way back to the States after the award ceremony, but, instead, the 36kg weight was caused by around 40 pairs of shoes he had packed for his eight-day trip. Mickey was made to redistribute his footwear among other cases before he was cleared for travel.

He wears plenty of bling on his fingers – sometimes

sporting four rings at a time – and even has some in his mouth, courtesy of a tooth capped in gold.

Mickey wears sunglasses and tinted spectacles everywhere – but that may have less to do with fashion choice and more to do with him having conjunctivitis. He got the condition, also known as pink-eye, from all the Vaseline and leather gloves slamming into his eyes during the boxing years and it tends to reappear when he gets his make-up done for movies. He is often seen sporting Sama's Press sunglasses but also likes Loree Rodkin and classic Ray-Ban Wayfarers.

Mickey's outfits may look like a haphazard series of unfortunate events, strange choices put together off the cuff, just like his award acceptance speeches, but a lot of thought actually goes into each ensemble. Even more thought since he started employing a stylist.

Michael Fisher was hired by Fox Searchlight to style Mickey during *The Wrestler*'s attention-grabbing press and publicity tour, but then remained with the star during awards season and beyond. Once Mickey realised Michael was willing to help him express his own style rather than impose radically different ideas, a thriving professional relationship was born.

Fisher, who has worked as an assistant to ace photographer Annie Leibovitz and leading stylist Rachel Zoe and provided fashion tips to the likes of Beyoncé Knowles and Kate Hudson, tweaked his client's look with additions and ideas while still making it innately Mickey. He and the star wanted the clothes Mickey wore to be as dramatic and memorable as his performance in *The Wrestler*. The first thing Mickey said to him was, 'I'm not George Clooney and I'm never going to be George Clooney,' a reference to that star priding himself on having worn the same Calvin Klein tuxedo to Hollywood events for years.

The play safe option of smart black suit with a white shirt as favoured by Clooney and countless other actors was never going to be for him. Mickey takes risks in his fashion choices just like he does in his roles. That strategy paid off with rebel Mickey's red carpet selections getting as much if not more attention than anything worn by actresses during the 2009 awards season. His butch, bizarre but brilliant outfits brought a kind of dishevelled elegance to showbiz events that made Mickey the talk of the fashion world as well as the film community. His dashing new look was variously described as 'Miami dandy', 'Modern Musketeer', 'Salvador Dali creepy', 'wacky and tacky', 'Toad of Toad Hall' and 'stolen from a Cirque du Soleil performer'. Crueller critics suggested the clothes were just a deliberate attempt to distract from whatever he had done to his face.

He may have been flying by the seat of his Dolce and Gabbana pants during the whole process but he was definitely being noticed and, with the stylist's assistance, Mickey's look clearly went from a bit of a mess to kind of cool.

As the awards season events turned into an endless parade of trophies for *Slumdog Millionaire* and Kate Winslet, the only tantalising suspense came from the question: what will Mickey Rourke wear next?

Mickey tended to stick to his favourite European designers, wearing Dolce to the BAFTAs and Screen Actors Guild awards, Billionaire Couture (owned by Formula One mogul Flavio Briatore) to the Golden Globes, Jean-Paul

Gaultier to the Paris première of *The Wrestler* and Gaultier again at the Oscars. He teamed all these stylish designer clothes of gold, silver, midnight blue and other striking colours with his macho outlaw accessories and somehow pulled it off. Nobody else could wear such a sartorial riot of different outfits and get away with them but Mickey managed it to become an unlikely trendsetter in the process. At the 2009 Oscars, he was the unanimous pick of fashion experts as best-dressed man thanks to his ivory Gaultier tuxedo accessorised with the pendant honouring his late dog, Loki.

Stylish rebel Mickey was so embraced by the fashion community that he landed a front-row seat at the 2009 New York Fashion Week show of designer Domenico Vacca, an Italian ex-lawyer-turned-red-hot designer. Mickey sat next to Forest Whitaker who had worn the designer's clothes when he picked up his Best Actor Oscar for *The Last King of Scotland*.

Mickey likes high-end clothes stores the way gamblers like betting shops and, during his many trips to London, has been a frequent visitor to the Harrods menswear department and the tailors of Savile Row. But he likes Italian designers best for the macho aesthetic they bring to their clothes.

Adding to the macho look are the seven tattoos Mickey has on his body, which include an American-Indian symbol for strength, an Oriental symbol for 'soul and spirit', a leopard's head with the Chinese ideogram for *Year of the Dragon* and also the words 'Carré Forever'.

Mickey attributes his lifelong interest in fashion to both his late grandmother, who was always a sharp dresser, and

his background in Miami, a trendsetting city where flamboyant styles were commonplace. After leaving school, he
did toy with the idea of studying either fashion or interior
design but his poor academic results made a college place
unlikely and he instead just hung out with his mates and
dressed in as cool a way as he could. His pride and joy back
then was a pair of handmade platform shoes in black and
pink. Mickey stands just under 6ft tall but in those crazy
things he looked 6ft 5in.

Around 1973, his absolute fashion icon was David
Bowie and Mickey would dress like the glam-rock hero in
stack-heeled boots, tight leather trousers and cut-off
shirts. The Ziggy Stardust wannabe even had green hair at
one point. When the pair became friends years later, the
pop star was thrilled to hear he had been such an influence
on Mickey's life.

Mickey loved David's music as well as his outfits. Bowie
thought his friend had some musical skills of his own and
even let him perform on one of his records. Mickey can be
heard performing a rap duet with David in the track
'Shining Star (Makin' My Love)' on the 1987 Bowie album
Never Let Me Down.

Around that time, Mickey had developed a particular
look of his own which made him a style icon around the
world – the black sunglasses, the cigarette drooping from
his lips, the unkempt hair, the stubble, stylish jackets and
black t-shirts . . . it was all about attitude and cool. Things
fell apart a little in the boxing years when the endless
hoodies and gym pants he wore back then were far from
glamorous. But then his mind was clearly much more on
fights than fashion.

In the wilderness years post-boxing and pre-comeback, he spent much of his time pumping iron and hanging out with bodybuilders at Gold's Gym in Venice, California, and his sweat-soaked fashions of the time reflected the company he was keeping rather than the movie star he aspired to become again. It is little wonder that agent David Unger ordered him to lose the gym clothes and smarten up as part of the career comeback strategy for his client.

He has tried out various looks in the last two decades – we've had hip-hop Mickey, biker Mickey and foppish Mickey among others. Through it all, he has stuck to two key rules that suit him – he never wears red and hardly ever wears underwear.

This mix of flamboyant but quality clothes and tough guy accessories he goes for now is an undoubtedly stylish combination. Darren Aronofsky has a theory that Mickey wears all these eye-catching outfits as a defence mechanism to stop people looking into his eyes – the windows to the soul. He has certainly hidden behind a mask or his characters in the past, but these days Mickey seems a whole lot happier and is just being himself – and looking good doing it.

Long may he continue to work the red carpet with panache, keep taking fashion chances and go on getting everyone talking with his decadent selections. It may not be to everyone's taste, but the man's certainly got style.

13

New Horizons

Mickey Rourke was over the moon when he was offered the main villain's role in *Iron Man 2* – until he saw how much he would be paid for the follow-up to a film which made half a billion dollars worldwide. The offer was $250,000 – a princely sum to most of us but an insultingly low one for an Oscar-nominated actor in a big-budget blockbuster.

Now Mickey had a dilemma. After *The Wrestler* had made him successful again, but not wealthy, he had resolved to chase the best roles rather than the best pay cheques – and he was extremely keen to act alongside Robert Downey Jr in the sequel to one of Hollywood's best recent hits. But even so, could he really let moneybags Marvel Entertainment get him on the cheap? They had already shown they wouldn't be held to ransom on this project by replacing Terrene Howard with Don Cheadle after Howard protested his pay deal for returning as the superhero's sidekick, Lt Col James Rhodes.

Talks continued for weeks as Marvel claimed money problems. But when their latest report showed huge fourth-quarter profits of $63 million, mostly due to DVD sales of the first *Iron Man* film, it was hard to keep making that argument. In the end, it took the personal intervention of Robert Downey Jr to persuade movie bosses to fork out more for Mickey. Like Mickey, he was a troubled but talented actor who had made a cool comeback and he knew the sequel would be a whole lot more special with Mickey in it. The deal was finally done in March 2009 – a month ahead of filming – with the increase in pay undisclosed but said to be substantial.

Mickey immediately dedicated himself to getting into character for his role – that of a tattooed Russian gangster named Ivan Vanko, who becomes the supervillain Whiplash.

He did it by flying to Moscow and visiting the notorious Butyrka prison, known for its brutal conditions and hardman inmates, where, with real dedication to duty, he had himself locked in a cell and manacled in an ancient torture device.

■　■　■

So, where next for Mickey Rourke? He looks like he has gone 12 rounds with a heavyweight champion and maybe several more with a cosmetic surgeon . . . but he's still in there punching. The odds would seem to be against him following up *The Wrestler* with more hit films and awards. After all, there are few lead roles for actors over 50 and Mickey's certainly got form for throwing away chances at lasting stardom. But he's also shown it's always wrong to count him out.

In his favour is the fact that Mickey occupies a unique place in the film business as just about the only star around right now who can convincingly play the vulnerable tough guy. He has the same tough-on-the-outside, tender-on-the inside quality which has characterised legends in

Hollywood history like Marlon Brando, Clark Gable and Humphrey Bogart.

Now that he's finally showing signs of understanding how showbusiness works, Mickey, together with his agent, is putting together a plan to keep his career hot and become a respected elder statesman of Hollywood. The idea is that he will carry on his much-improved work ethic by being consistent in his performances and professionalism, only select movies with integrity, work just with directors he respects and co-stars he likes, and not shoot his mouth off so much. If he can achieve all that, then Mickey should remain a major figure in movies for a long time.

He is busier than ever with a string of intriguing projects lined up that are designed to work towards his goal. Only time will tell if *The Wrestler* is likely to be the final great performance which caps his career or just the start of a new era of terrific Rourke roles. But the latter does look achievable judging by the range of films he has lined up for 2010 and 2011.

First to be released looks likely to be the crime thriller *13*, which Mickey calls a 'wonderful' film. He plays anti-hero Jesse James Jefferson, a tobacco-chewing Texan cowboy and ex-convict who becomes embroiled in a version of Russian roulette where high rollers bet on the lives of kidnapped outsiders. Jason Statham, Ray Winstone, Ray Liotta and 50 Cent make up an impressive ensemble cast. Also in the film is one of Mickey's oldest and dearest friends, larger-than-life Hell's Angel-turned-bodyguard-turned-actor and DJ Chuck Zito, who appears as one of the gang who kidnap Jefferson so he can be a player in the deadly game.

There's an even more intriguing group around him in

the rip-roaring adventure movie *The Expendables*, due out in April 2010. Action stars Sylvester Stallone, Jet Li, Dolph Lundgren and Jason Statham – yet again – play a group of macho, neck-snapping mercenaries planning to topple a South American dictator and Mickey co-stars as an unscrupulous arms dealer, named Tool, who provides the weapons for this brawny band of brothers. Old pal Eric Roberts will play a CIA agent and, adding to the line-up of action stars in the movie, California Governor Arnold Schwarzenegger has a cameo role as himself.

May 2010 sees the worldwide release of surefire blockbuster *Iron Man 2* – the biggest film Mickey Rourke has ever made. The sequel to the 2008 superhero smash-hit sees Robert Downey Jr returning in the title role and Mickey as his new nemesis, Russian supervillain Whiplash. Also along for the thrill ride are Scarlett Johansson in tight leather outfits as femme fatale Black Widow and Sam Rockwell as rival industrialist Justin Hammer. But it was Mickey's casting as the main villain which got all the attention.

Director Jon Favreau picked Mickey for the role because he knew the bad guy had to be a compelling figure and there were few more compelling actors around than him. Mickey told Favreau that he didn't want to play the character as a one-dimensional villian and instead would like to inject some humour into the role. That's how Vanko came to have a pet cockatoo who he speaks to while building the metal whiplash suit. To play the part, Mickey had to lose the extra weight he had put on for *The Wrestler* and learn a Russian dialect, neither of which was easy. Nor was getting comfortable in his armoured suit costume for the film, which weighed 23lb.

While Downey's character, Tony Stark, is completely encased in his metal suit, Whiplash has a half-suit of metal and leather showing off plenty of skin along with lots of Russian prison tattoos coating his flesh. His hands and torso are wrapped in metal braces sporting neat weapons like electrified whips as well as a glowing power pack chest device similar to the one Iron Man uses.

The pair's on screen showdown is set to be the highlight of 2010's summer blockbusters and Mickey had the time of his life filming the movie. He was back in the big time and had the respect of everyone he was working with. He also admits that further tough guy roles like Whiplash are a more likely future for him than romantic leads, saying, 'I'm not 30 years old so I don't get the girl any more, unless I cut the guy's head off and take her.'

The first footage from *Iron Man 2* was screened to 6,500 deliriously approving fans – many of whom had camped out overnight to get in to see it – at San Diego comic-con on 25 July, 2009. There was an instant buzz about Rourke's scenes and the film's director and leading man spoke warmly at that event about Mickey.

Jan Favreau said: 'We informed Mickey that the character he would be playing was of Russian descent and had been in jail over there and the next thing I heard, he was in a Russian prison researching the part. I learned about it from TMZ. It turns out he was a sex god in Russia because the first film they got over there after Perestroika was *9½ weeks*!'

Robert Downey Jr joked, 'Where else do you want to go if you're a sex god in Russia except a prison?!' Asked about getting to work with Mickey, Robert said, 'I barely know what to say. I thought I was eccentric! But he's something else.'

There are a number of other interesting Mickey Rourke projects to come after *Iron Man 2*. Mickey will be hoping for more *9½ Weeks*-type steamy success with erotic drama *11 Minutes*, based on the bestselling Paulo Coehlo novel. This one sees Mickey as the owner of a Geneva gentleman's club which is home to Switzerland's finest call girls.

After that, *St Vincent* is to find him starring as a hit-man who disguises himself as a priest and ends up taking the confession of his target. The action thriller will reunite him with director Walter Hill who was behind the camera on *Johnny Handsome*.

He also has a dramatic lead role lined up in *Passion Plays* as a down-on-his-luck 1950s trumpet player who encounters an angel, played by *Transformers* sexpot Megan Fox.

Other possible projects he has been linked with include *Broken Horses*, a Bollywood-meets-Hollywood gangster drama; *Seven Holes for Air*, a Western in which he might act alongside *Sopranos* star James Gandolfini; *Sin City 2* is often talked about, and Mickey hopes to film *Wild Horses*, which it has taken him the past 18 years to write, about two long-estranged brothers taking a motorbiking trip together.

There are no comedies among his upcoming pictures – in fact, he hasn't fronted any comedy films in his entire career, as that's something he's had no desire to tackle. But dramas are a different matter and, striking while the iron's hot, he's got them stacked up one after another.

Mickey also made time in his packed schedule to make an emotional visit in June 2009 to the place that helped make him the great actor he is today – the Actors' Studio. He went back to be interviewed about his career for an episode of acclaimed US cable TV series *Inside The Actors' Studio* – and was touched by the warm reception from current students who hung on his every word. He took time afterwards to shake plenty of hands and talk to the audience, humbly accepting congratulations on his comeback and their best wishes for the many movies ahead of him.

That same month, he was the toast of Spike TV's Guy Awards where his victory as Guy of the Year was loudly celebrated by a host of fellow stars including Quentin Tarantino, Brad Pitt, Ben Stiller, Halle Berry and Clint Eastwood. Sacha Baron Cohen was also there, appearing in character as Bruno to pay an amusing tribute by cheekily joking, 'Mickey Rourke was so sexy in *The Wrestler* as a broken-down piece of meat – which is, coincidentally, what I had in my hand at the end of that movie.'

Mickey no longer looked out of place in such A-list company. After years of struggle to get back to this point, he was a genuine movie star once again. Clearly, the days of waiting for the phone to ring with film offers are long gone. Thanks to behaving himself, thanks to therapy and especially thanks to *The Wrestler*, he has the chance to work on a string of hugely promising projects.

Now that his career is no longer a train wreck, the task now is to make the most of this long-awaited opportunity. He is determined not to mess it up. Mickey says, 'I was out of the game so many years and didn't realise it would take this long to get back. But there ain't no quit in me and I'm grateful to have this chance now. I appreciate it a lot that people trust me again after me raising hell for years. But I know this is my last chance. I'm not going to have another one. I'll always have that little man inside me with two axes but I've got to learn to keep him the fuck quiet.'

But you can banish any thoughts that this more serious and mild-mannered Mickey is dispensing with his dangerous and eccentric sides. A look around the contents of his New York home will confirm that. Mickey is now back living in Greenwich Village and journalist Steve Garbarino visited the star's rented townhouse as part of an excellent profile of the actor for *Maxim* magazine – and found it to be a place of fascinating contrasts. As well as ornate chandeliers, a marble fireplace and fancy furniture, the home contains a loaded handgun, a stripper's pole and a rubber dildo suction-cupped to a wall. There's also a punch bag, portraits of Loki, Carré Otis and Richard Harris, and plenty of prescription pills.

Mickey regularly invites friends round for Mexican nights where they eat take-out tacos and burritos washed down with Corona beers. When he fancies something grander, celebrity-packed restaurant The Waverly Inn is just two streets away.

During all the years he lived in Los Angeles, Mickey never knew his neighbours, but now he is seemingly on first-name terms with everyone in the neighbourhood. Happy in his home life and content in his career, it's a triumphant turnaround in fortunes for the film star.

Many movie fans had watched in dismay as Mickey's promising career imploded and his riches to rags story can be see as a cautionary tale for up-and-coming actors. But the way he turned things around can only be admired. His posse pushed off and his wives walked out but Mickey's talent never left him. That was clear from his acting in *The Wrestler*, a piece of work which revived memories of other spellbinding performances for which Mickey Rourke deserves a place among the acting greats.

He could get one, too, if an ongoing campaign by fans to get Mickey his own star on the Hollywood Walk of Fame proves successful. The Oscar nominee certainly seems more deserving than several of the actors selected for that particular honour in 2010, such as Jon Cryer, Sam Waterston and Mark Wahlberg. And those loyal Mickey Rourke fans are suddenly everywhere now – from Facebook to MySpace – and spreading the word on lovingly maintained websites like UniquelyRourke.com.

After some lonely years, Mickey has more friends in his life now, and ones who are a positive influence. Among them is fellow Oscar-nominee Brad Pitt, who shares his enthusiasm for motorbikes. Mickey can't afford to buy the really expensive ones Brad owns, but enjoys chatting about bikes with the heart-throb superstar.

Mickey's wild, high-octane life appears to be calming down at last and heading in the right direction. He is still in therapy, although his appointments are down to one visit or phone call a week. He is still in regular contact with Father Peter and always has Christmas dinner with him at the church rectory. And Mickey continues to pray – no longer for himself but now for the safety of his dogs, whom he has been missing terribly while being away so often lately filming.

Mickey is still wrestling with his demons, but it's a fight he seems to be winning. Randy 'The Ram' Robinson couldn't give himself a future in *The Wrestler* – but it certainly looks like the movie has given Mickey a very bright one.

Filmography

Film Roles

1941 (1979)
Role: Private Reese
Director: Steven Spielberg
Co-star: John Belushi

Fade to Black (1980)
Role: Richie
Director: Vernon Zimmerman
Co-star: Denis Christopher

Heaven's Gate (1980)
Role: Nick Ray
Director: Michael Cimino
Co-star: Kris Kristofferson

Body Heat (1981)
Role: Teddy Lewis
Director: Lawrence Kasdan
Co-star: William Hurt

Diner (1982)
Role: Robert 'Boogie' Sheftell
Director: Barry Levinson
Co-star: Steve Guttenberg

Eureka (1983)
Role: Aurelio D'Amato
Director: Nicolas Roeg
Co-star: Gene Hackman

Rumble Fish (1983)
Role: Motorcycle Boy
Director: Francis Ford Coppola
Co-star: Matt Dillon

The Pope of Greenwich Village (1984)
Role: Charlie Moran
Director: Stuart Rosenberg
Co-star: Eric Roberts

Year of the Dragon (1985)
Role: Captain Stanley White
Director: Michael Cimino
Co-star: John Lone

9½ Weeks (1986)
Role: John Gray
Director: Adrian Lyne
Co-star: Kim Basinger

Angel Heart (1987)
Role: Harry Angel
Director: Alan Parker
Co-star: Robert De Niro

Barfly (1987)

Role: Henry Chinaski
Director: Barbet Shroeder
Co-star: Faye Dunaway

A Prayer for the Dying (1987)

Role: Martin Fallon
Director: Mike Hodges
Co-star: Bob Hoskins

Homeboy (1988)

Role: Johnny Walker
Director: Michael Seresin
Co-star: Christopher Walken

Franceso (1989)

Role: Francesco, aka Francis of Assisi
Director: Liliana Cavani
Co-star: Helena Bonham Carter

Johnny Handsome (1989)

Role: John Sedley, aka Johnny Mitchell
Director: Walter Hill
Co-star: Morgan Freeman

Wild Orchid (1989)

Role: James Wheeler
Director: Zalman King
Co-star: Carré Otis

Desperate Hours (1990)

Role: Michael Bosworth
Director: Michael Cimino
Co-star: Anthony Hopkins

Harley Davidson and the Marlboro Man (1991)

Role: Harley
Director: Simon Wincer
Co-star: Don Johnson

White Sands (1992)

Role: Gorman Lennox
Director: Roger Donaldson
Co-star: Willem Dafoe

F.T.W. (1993)

Role: Frank T. Wells
Director: Michael Kerbelnikoff
Co-star: Lori Singer

Fall Time (1995)

Role: Florence
Director: Paul Warner
Co-star: Stephen Baldwin

Exit in Red (1996)

Role: Ed Altman
Director: Yurek Bogayevicz
Co-star: Anthony Michael Hall

Bullet (1996)

Role: Butch 'Bullet' Stein
Director: Julien Temple
Co-star: Tupac Shakur

Double Team (1997)

Role: Stavros
Director: Tsui Hark
Co-star: Jean Claude Van Damme

Another 9½ Weeks (1997)

Role: John Gray
Director: Anne Goursaud
Co-star: Angie Everhart

The Rainmaker (1997)

Role: Bruiser Stone
Director: Francis Ford Coppola
Co-star: Matt Damon

Buffalo '66 (1998)

Role: The Bookie
Director: Vincent Gallo
Co-star: Vincent Gallo

Point Blank (1998)

Role: Rudy Ray
Director: Max Earl Beesley
Co-star: Danny Trejo

Thursday (1998)
Role: Kasarov
Director: Skip Woods
Co-star: Thomas Jane

Cousin Joey (1999)
Role: Brother
Director: Sante D'Orazio
Co-star: Jaye Davidson

Shergar (1999)
Role: Gavin O'Rourke
Director: Dennis Lewiston
Co-star: Ian Holm

Out in Fifty (1999)
Role: Jack Bracken
Director: Bojesse Christopher
Co-star: Christina Applegate

Shades (1999)
Role: Paul S. Sullivan
Director: Eric Van Looy
Co-star: Gene Bervoets

Animal Factory (2000)
Role: Jan The Actress
Director: Steve Buscemi
Co-star: Edward Furlong

Get Carter (2000)

Role:	Cyrus Paice
Director:	Stephen Kay
Co-star:	Sylvester Stallone

The Pledge (2001)

Role:	James Olstad
Director:	Sean Penn
Co-star:	Jack Nicholson

They Crawl (2001)

Role:	Tiny Frakes
Director:	John Allardice
Co-star:	Tamara Davies

Picture Claire (2001)

Role:	Eddie
Director:	Bruce McDonald
Co-star:	Juliette Lewis

Spun (2002)

Role:	The Cook
Director:	Jonas Akerlund
Co-star:	Jason Schwartzman

Masked and Anonymous (2003)

Role:	Edmund
Director:	Larry Charles
Co-star:	Bob Dylan

Once Upon a Time in Mexico (2003)
Role: Billy Chambers
Director: Robert Rodriguez
Co-star: Antonio Banderas

Man on Fire (2004)
Role: Jordan Kalfus
Director: Tony Scott
Co-star: Denzel Washington

Sin City (2005)
Role: Marv
Director: Robert Rodriguez
Co-star: Jessica Alba

Domino (2005)
Role: Ed Moseby
Director: Tony Scott
Co-star: Keira Knightley

Stormbreaker (2006)
Role: Darrius Sayle
Director: Geoffrey Sax
Co-star: Alex Pettyfer

The Wrestler (2008)
Role: Randy 'The Ram' Robinson
Director: Darren Aronofsky
Co-star: Marisa Tomei

Killshot (2009)
Role: Armand 'The Blackbird' Degas
Director: John Madden
Co-star: Diane Lane

The Informers (2009)
Role: Peter
Director: Gregor Jordan
Co-star: Kim Basinger

13 (2010)
Role: Jefferson
Director: Gela Babluani
Co-star: Jason Statham

The Expendables (2010)
Role: Tool
Director: Sylvester Stallone
Co-star: Sylvester Stallone

Iron Man 2 (2010)
Role: Ivan/Whiplash
Director: Jon Favreau
Co-star: Robert Downey Jr

Television Roles
City in Fear (1980)
Role: Tony Pate

Act of Love (1980)
Role: Joseph Cybulkowski

Rape and Marriage: The Rideout Case (1980)
Role: John Rideout

Hardcase (1981)
Role: Perk Dawson

The Last Outlaw (1993)
Role: Graff

Thicker Than Blood (1998)
Role: Father Frank Larkin

*WrestleMania **XXV*** (2009)
Role: Himself

Screenplays
(as 'Sir' Eddie Cook)
Homeboy (1988)
F.T.W. (1994)
Bullet (1996)

Major Awards
Golden Globe – Best Actor (Drama) – *The Wrestler*
BAFTA Film Award – Best Actor – *The Wrestler*
Independent Spirit Award – Best Actor – *The Wrestler*
Saturn Award – Best Supporting Actor – *Sin City*
National Society of Film Critics – Best Supporting
Actor – *Diner*
Academy Award Nomination for Best Actor – *The Wrestler*

Video Game Voiceovers

Driv3r (2004)
Role: Jericho

True Crime: New York City (2005)
Role: Terry Higgins

Rogue Warrior: Black Razor (2009)
Role: Richard 'Demo Dick' Marcinko

Japanese TV Commercials

Suntory, Lark and Daihatsu

Pop Video Appearances

Enrique Iglesias ('Hero') 2001
John Rich ('Shuttin' Detroit Down') 2009

Music

Provided the mid-song rap on the David Bowie song 'Shining Star (Makin' My Love)' which was on the 1987 Bowie album *Never Let Me Down*
Music supervisor on the 1996 film *Bullet*